Be as Happy as Your Dog

Be as Happy as Your Dog

16 Dog-Tested Ways To Be Happier Using Pawsitive Psychology

Michelle Waitzman

5FOOT
COMMUNICATIONS

Copyright © 2023 Michelle Waitzman

All rights reserved. No part of this book may be used or reproduced in any manner whatsoever without written permission of the author, except in the case of brief quotations in critical articles and reviews.

For media or speaking requests, permissions, or bulk purchases, contact the author at contact@beashhappyasyourdog.com

Published 2023, 1st edition

Cover photo: Samantha Rose Photography "Meatball"
Back cover photos: Amy Morris "Maya"; Kim McFadden "Abbie"; Patricia Simmons "Ziggy Lulu"; Janice Campbell "Princess Lily"; Megan Love "Rush"
Author photo: Margot Daley Photography
Cover design: Michelle Fairbanks for Fresh Design
Interior design: Sophie Hanks

Subjects (BISAC): SELF-HELP–Personal Growth–Happiness; SELF-HELP–Motivational & Inspirational; PETS–Dogs–General

ISBN: 978-1-7387874-0-1 (paperback)

ISBN: 978-1-7387874-1-8 (e-book)

To Marlowe and Nuka, my happiness role models

Contents

Introduction	1
1. Learn new tricks	13
2. Live in the moment	25
3. Wag your tail	39
4. Never stop playing	51
5. Find your pack	65
6. Trust the "sniff test"	77
7. Bark, don't bite	91
8. Shake it off	103
9. Go for a walk	115
10. Stop and smell things	127
11. Enjoy some treats	141
12. Accept praise	153
13. Play fetch	165
14. Chase the uncatchable	177
15. Curl up and sleep	189
16. Dig below the surface	201
Stay pawsitive!	211
Selected bibliography	215
Notes	217
Acknowledgments	233
About the author	235

Photo credit: Shelley Tremere "Ozzy"

Introduction

Pawsitive dogma

Dogs instinctively understand that there is much they can learn from humans. Only the wisest humans understand they have just as much to learn from dogs.

Why dogs are great role models for happiness

If you've picked up this book, you're probably a dog lover. And if you're a dog lover, you've noticed how dogs approach life: they take every opportunity to enjoy whatever comes their way—a chance to play, walk, eat, cuddle, or sleep. They are always ready to show you how happy they are and how much they enjoy being with you, and they aren't busy fretting over things that happened in the past or that might happen in the future. A dog's default position is to be happy—right here, right now.

If you can adopt a more dog-like attitude in your own life, you could become happy by default too. That's what I hope this book will teach you. I take a close look at 16 things that most dogs do and explain what we can learn from them with the help of both dog experts and happiness experts. The result is a collection of suggestions for adding more happiness to your life.

What connects us to dogs?

People's special connection to dogs is not new. We have been living side by side for around 30,000 years, according to most estimates. That's a long-term relationship of epic proportions. Dogs have evolved to understand our actions and emotions, and to make us care about them so we provide food and shelter, as well as companionship.

These days, dogs are not just working animals or an amusement for children—they are family; they share our homes and, in many cases, our couches and beds. According to surveys of dog and cat owners, 90% of us consider our pets to be members of the family and 83% of us refer to ourselves as our pet's "mom" or "dad." I actually call myself their "mommy," but you get the picture.

Even without this book, living with a dog may help you to be happier, calmer, and healthier, according to research on the effects of dogs on our physical and mental health. Over the past few decades, interacting with dogs has been proven to relieve your anxiety, lower your blood pressure, help you lose weight, and reduce your chances of cardiovascular disease, among other things.

Researchers have also been hard at work trying to understand much more about how dogs think, feel, and learn. Their work has revealed that people and dogs have much more in common than we used to believe. Dogs' brains have many of the same structures and functions as ours, so the same areas are used to process emotions, memories, information, and so on. They also produce the same hormones and undergo the same chemical changes in their brains that we do when they feel stress, fear, joy, fulfillment, and affection. Knowing this, it becomes easy to see how looking at the world through a dog's eyes (and nose) can show us pathways to happiness that apply to two-leggers like you and me.

Why are dogs happier than people?

The things that make dogs happy and the things that make people happy are pretty similar: spending quality time with friends and family, eating good food, participating in activities they enjoy, checking out interesting places, getting better at things they like doing, and relaxing in a safe, comfortable place.

On the other hand, the list of things that make dogs unhappy is very short: pain, fear, loneliness, hunger, and boredom pretty much cover it. Our lists can be almost endless. On top of the things dogs get unhappy about, we have career pressures, social anxiety, fear of missing out, unrealistic expectations of how we should look, the desire to impress others, financial problems, envy of other people's lives, bitterness about people who wronged us in the past, and fear of what might happen in the future—and that's just for starters.

When a dog is unhappy, it lasts for about as long as the immediate cause. Once they're no longer in pain, afraid, lonely, hungry, or bored, they generally get right back to being happy and embracing the good things in their life. Dogs are experts at letting go of negative feelings. We're not so good at this. In fact, we can feel bad about a negative experience for years.

This is because our own brains work against us. People have something called a "negativity bias." Throughout our evolution, it was important for us to pay more attention to things that made us unsafe or threatened our position in the community. As a result, we notice those negative things more, remember them better, think about them more, and make our decisions based on them. Just to cancel out your negativity bias, it's estimated that you need to have *nine times* as many positive thoughts as negative ones.

Finding new ways to have more of those positive thoughts, and dwell less on the negative ones, is the only way to increase your happiness. That's what the suggestions in this book will help you do.

How will this book make you happier?

There are thousands of self-help books out there. How will this one make you happier? I've presented the advice in this book in a way that makes sense to dog lovers. You may have read other books and found that the suggestions didn't work for you or didn't align with your beliefs and values—you just couldn't connect with them. Self-help only works when you read it and think, "Of course! That makes so much sense."

Even within this book, some chapters may light up your mind more than others. Feel free to ignore what doesn't work for you and try the parts you're excited about. My goal is for some of the suggestions to inspire you to make changes and motivate you to live a happier life. The great thing is this isn't an all-or-nothing program you have to follow. You can't get it wrong. If something isn't working for you, just move on to a different suggestion.

What is positive psychology?

I've based my advice in this book on a field of research called positive psychology (but I call it "pawsitive psychology"—because dogs!). The field was popularized in the 1990s by a psychologist and professor named Martin Seligman. The idea behind positive psychology is that researchers should not limit themselves to studying psychological problems and how to treat them. They should work equally hard to find out how all people can thrive and reach their full potential, including maximizing their happiness.

Although it's a relatively new field, the research in positive psychology has consistently found that everyday people can use a variety of techniques and approaches to have happier, more fulfilling lives.

Is your happiness within your control?

Not everyone is starting this journey from the same place. You might have some friends who seem to be happy most of the time, while others are constantly grumpy and pessimistic. It turns out that each of us has a baseline happiness level. You can become happier than your baseline, but generally that doesn't last long before you return to "normal." The same thing happens when something makes you more unhappy than usual. Once it passes, you usually go back to your baseline happiness level quite quickly.

So why even bother trying to become happier? Because there are things you can do to move your baseline. About 50% of your baseline happiness level is determined by your genes, and another 10% is determined by your environment and circumstances—things you can't easily control. But that leaves 40% of your baseline happiness level to be determined by your actions and the choices you make. That means you can improve your baseline happiness by choosing to do the things that make you happier more often.

Meet my dogs

You'll be reading a lot about (and from) my two dogs throughout this book. I thought you might like to meet them before we get started.

Marlowe

Marlowe was the first dog we adopted, at around five months old, early in 2014. He was born on a First Nations reserve in Ontario, Canada. When he and his littermates were just five weeks old, their mother was hit by a car and didn't survive. The litter was rescued by an organization that placed them in foster homes until they were old enough to be adopted. Marlowe was the last to be adopted because he was shy and a bit anxious. He's a very fluffy, large, white mixed breed (likely with husky or malamute as the dominant breed) with a bushy, curled tail and small, floppy, tan ears.

Marlowe has always been a bit of an old soul. He doesn't play as much as most dogs, but he loves getting attention from people. He's very smart and recognizes a pretty impressive number of words and names. Marlowe is the thoughtful one, the cautious one.

Nuka

Nuka has gone through pretty much everything life can throw at a dog, and decided to be happy anyway. She's a fairly large, tan mixed breed who looks like a more delicate version of a yellow lab. She has a straight, thick tail and big, droopy ears. Nuka has the world's softest fur.

We don't know how Nuka's life began, but she was rescued at three or four months old with three littermates, all found in a dumpster. They were underweight and likely mistreated and abandoned. We adopted her about six months after we got Marlowe, since we wanted both our dogs to be at around the same stage in their lives. Nuka was a happy, playful puppy who loved having a big brother in Marlowe. When she was around

10 months old, we discovered that a rare parasite had destroyed one of her kidneys. The kidney had to be removed. Around age two she developed pain in both her knees and underwent knee surgeries one year apart, but her knees still get sore after a long walk. A year after that, a mysterious autoimmune reaction dropped the platelet level in her blood so low that any small wound would have caused her to bleed to death.

Throughout all of this, and most recently skin cancer, Nuka's default state has been to be happy and love her life. Every walk, every meal, every game, and every visitor is a cause for celebration. She is a wonderful role model for how to be happy, no matter what. Without a doubt, Nuka is my main inspiration for this book.

Meet the experts

I'm a lifelong dog lover, and I have always marveled at their embodiment of pure joy. I've learned a lot from my dogs over the past nine years (and from my previous dogs during my childhood). I've also sought out a lot of information about dog behavior, social structures, emotional expressions, and other secrets to their happiness in an effort to be a better "dog mom." Writing this book has given me a great excuse to dive even deeper into the canine mind and learn important lessons to apply to my own life and make me happier—and to share those lessons with you, of course.

Although my dogs provide the inspiration for this book, they're better at leading by example than providing their detailed points of view or explaining the latest research. For that, we'll need to rely on human expertise. So, all the suggestions in the next 16 chapters are based on research and advice from experts in the fields of dog behavior and positive psychology. I interviewed several of them and studied books and articles by others. Check out the selected bibliography at the end of this book if you want to do some further reading yourself. In the meantime, meet the smarty-pants experts you'll be hearing from throughout the book.

The dog experts

Nicole Barnett is a force-free, positive reinforcement dog trainer who runs a training and consulting business called We Work for Treats. She spoke to me from her home in Ontario, Canada.

Dr. John Bradshaw is an anthrozoologist who spent his academic career studying the interactions between animals and humans. He wrote the bestselling books *Dog Sense* and *Cat Sense*.

Dr. Stanley Coren is a psychology professor and leading dog behavior expert. His books include *Do Dogs Dream?*, *Why Does My Dog Act That Way?*, and *How to Speak Dog*. He spoke to me from his home in British Columbia, Canada.

Dr. Ian Dunbar is a veterinarian who popularized "lure and reward" training, which helped launch the positive reinforcement training movement. He founded his own dog training academy and has authored many books including *Before and After Getting Your Puppy* and *Dog Behavior*.

Dr. **Alexandra Horowitz** is a professor of psychology and a dog behavior expert. Her books include the bestselling *Inside of a Dog* about dog behavior and *On Looking* about human attention, so she's something of a crossover expert on both dogs and people.

The happiness experts

Shawn Achor is an author, speaker, and positive psychology advocate. He regularly speaks at Fortune 500 companies about the link between happiness and success. His books include *The Happiness Advantage* and *Before Happiness*.

Dr. Stuart Brown is a psychology researcher and the founder of the National Institute for Play. He authored the bestselling book *Play*, and his research on the importance of play in human development, success, and happiness has made him the leader in this field.

Dr. Katherine Compitus is a licensed clinical social worker, doctor of social welfare, and animal behavior scientist. She includes dogs in many of her therapy sessions with clients. She is also the founder and chair of Surrey Hills Sanctuary, a nonprofit organization that provides veterinary social work services. She spoke to me from her home in New York, USA.

Dr. Mihaly Csikszentmihalyi is a positive psychology pioneer who is best known for his research on "flow" (and his book of the same name) and its role in psychological well-being.

Oonagh Duncan is a fitness and wellness expert who cultivates healthy habits to help her clients transform through her business, Fit Feels Good. She is the author of *Healthy as F*ck* (published in the United States as *Ditch the Diet*).

Bridget Grenville-Cleave is the director of Workmad Ltd., which helps organizations and individuals improve their performance using applied positive psychology. She is a founding member of the International Positive Psychology Association and author of the book *Positive Psychology: A Toolkit for Happiness, Purpose and Well-being*.

Dr. Jonathan Haidt is a social psychologist and professor of ethical leadership. His books include *The Happiness Hypothesis* and *The Righteous Mind*.

Dr. Rick Hanson is a psychologist, positive neuroplasticity expert, and senior fellow of the Greater Good Science Center. His books include *Hardwiring Happiness*, *Resilient*, and *Buddha's Brain*.

Dr. Emma Seppälä is a psychologist and research scientist whose expertise is the science of happiness, emotional intelligence, and social connection. She lectures at the Yale School of Management. She is the author of the bestselling book *The Happiness Track*.

Stephanie Staples is a motivational speaker and life coach with a background in nursing. She hosted the radio show *Your Life Unlimited* for 12 years. She spoke to me from her home in British Columbia, Canada.

Kim Strobel is a happiness coach and motivational speaker who uses positive psychology and the latest research to empower educators. She is also a passionate advocate of animal rescue and has filled a gap in her community by rescuing hundreds of homeless or unwanted animals. She spoke to me from her home in Indiana, USA.

Photo credit: Katryn B. for Pixabay

1
Learn new tricks

Pawsitive dogma

If you want to change your life, you'll have to learn some new things. Change starts inside you.

Message from Marlowe

Learning new tricks is no big deal—anyone can do it, even an "old dog" like me! The important thing is to keep doing it over and over until it becomes easy, and keep those treats coming. In fact, if you do a trick over and over for long enough (like, every day for a few weeks) it turns into a habit and you don't even need to think about it. You just do it! To get to that point, you need a positive attitude and tons of encouragement. And treats. Did I mention treats?

That's how I learn to do new things: consistency, practice, and encouragement. You can do the same for yourself. In fact, if you want to make any big changes in your life, you'll have to. Learning new tricks or habits can take you in the direction you want to go—the direction that's going to make you happier.

What the dog experts say

Why do dogs bother learning how to do new things? Generally, dogs have three possible motivations to learn a new trick:

1. *It solves a problem for them.* Maybe your dog can smell treats inside a treat-dispensing ball, but the hole is too small to stick their tongue inside and eat them. Learning to roll the ball until the treats drop out solves the problem of being unable to get to the treats.
2. *They get a reward for it.* Positive reinforcement training is the method of choice for most dog trainers these days because dogs are very reward driven. If they get a treat or get to play with a toy after doing something, they'll happily learn to do it on command.
3. *It feels good.* Dogs seek our approval. We've bred that desire into them over thousands of years. So when they get something right and we get excited about it, they feel good about doing it.

Do these motivations sound familiar? If you think about it, people learn new things for the same reasons. It gets us closer to our goals by solving our problems, it brings us a reward we want, or it gives us a feeling of pride and accomplishment as well as approval from people who matter to us. And just like dogs, we love getting different kinds of rewards. Anthrozoologist John Bradshaw says, "Food can be an important reward, but dogs are unusual in that most also regard contact with their owner as rewarding in itself. Some types of dog also find the opportunity to go exploring and/or hunting as rewarding in its own right. Others find play rewarding in itself."

Learning new tricks is also fun simply because it's new. Dogs are more interested in new things, just like people are. They spend most of their time in the same home doing the same things every day. Any change is mentally stimulating. Dog behavior expert Alexandra Horowitz says, "Happiness is novelty—new toys, new treats—in a safe, well-known place. It can be a cure for boredom, too: the new requires attention and prompts activity. You need only watch the exuberance of an agility dog on a new course to see how good *new* is."

Learning to do something in a new context is also a new trick. Dog trainer Nicole Barnett says people don't always understand this when they're training their dogs. "A lot of people say, 'They sit at home but they can't sit at the park. They should know this.' But 'sit at home' is different from 'sit at the park.' It's a completely different skill."

Maybe you're good at resisting dessert at home, but not when you're eating out or at a party. Maybe you listen attentively to your team members at work, but you tend to tune out your family members at home. When you learn a new trick, learning to do it in different places and contexts takes extra practice. Don't be mad at yourself for needing some time to expand a new behavior and make it work everywhere, all the time. And don't be mad at your dog for knowing how to do something at home but forgetting it at the park or in the car.

> For a couple of years, I took Marlowe and Nuka to a local park every morning, where a bunch of dogs gathered to play while their humans caught up on the neighborhood happenings. One of the regulars often had a pocketful of treats that he distributed to all the dogs. The dogs learned to gather round and wait for him to toss them a treat. Marlowe had already learned that to get a treat from me—no matter where we were—he needed to sit down. So while all the other dogs clamored around, Marlowe would sit for his treat. When he realized other dogs were getting in front of him, he'd kind of scootch forward with his bum pointed at the ground, so that he was getting closer to the guy with the treats, but still succeeding at "sit."

What the happiness experts say

Most of us have goals and ambitions, things we'd like to learn or improve that we think would give us better lives. Since you're reading this book, you probably want to learn how to be happier! As you will discover, that can be learned just like anything else.

Let's talk about "learning" happiness for a moment. You might think you can't learn happiness because it depends on things that are out of your control. To some extent, that's true. As I mentioned earlier, we all have a baseline level of happiness. We get happier than our baseline when good things happen, and sadder than our baseline when bad things happen, but we tend to return to our natural level pretty fast.

So how can you learn to become happier? You need to focus on the 40% of your happiness baseline that lies within your control—determined by your actions and attitude. That's how adopting a more dog-like approach to life can make a real difference in how happy you are, regardless of the baseline you started with.

Learning new tricks usually requires a change from what you're used to. This is hard for most people, because we're comfortable with our routines, and we don't like to admit that we've been getting things wrong for so long. Health and fitness expert Oonagh Duncan says, "A lot of people will tell you that they are an easygoing, go-with-the-flow type person, until you ask them to go with a different flow than the one they are used to." We tend to suffer from the "sunken costs" fallacy, where the more time and effort we've put into something, the less likely we are to admit that it was a mistake. So the first step to learning new tricks is to be willing to change something about your life—or at least your routine.

To reinforce your new tricks (or habits) so that you stick with them, you need to feel good about them. According to social psychologist Jonathan Haidt, you feel good when you accomplish something or learn something, which reinforces your behavior and puts you in a more positive mindset where "hard work becomes effortless. We want to keep exerting ourselves, honing our skills, using our strengths."

That feeling of hard work becoming effortless is called "flow," a term coined by researcher Mihaly Csikszentmihalyi. He found that once you start getting good at something you enjoy, you become immersed in it and lose track of time because the activity itself is so satisfying. Flow creates a feeling of accomplishment and mastery that lifts your mood. In fact, Csikszentmihalyi claims that flow is associated with our strongest feelings of happiness. How do you feel when you're in the middle of doing something you really enjoy and think you're doing well? Do you feel like you could happily keep doing it all day? Whether it's something as simple as baking cookies or going for a run, or as complex as solving equations or playing in an orchestra—that's often when you're at your happiest.

Learning new tricks throughout life is also a great way to stay mentally healthy. When you make your brain work on figuring out new problems or challenges, your neurons literally make new connections with one another. This ability to constantly rewire our brains is called "neuroplasticity," and it keeps working for as long as you keep exercising your brain with new challenges. People who stop trying to learn things and expand their minds begin to feel old, bored, and depressed. People who keep active and try new things, even as they grow older, tend to feel much happier and stay healthier.

I grew up shy—even making a phone call to a stranger was difficult for me. So it's not surprising that public speaking was one of my worst fears. The idea of standing in front of a big group of people, potentially embarrassing myself or being painfully boring, would tie my stomach in knots. But as my career took various twists and turns, I realized that I had things to share, and that being able to connect with more people at once would make me happier. At a conference, I attended a presentation on how to create better presentations. Afterward, I told the presenter, "I've decided that I'm going to make myself do a presentation at next year's conference." Having said it out loud, I felt committed to learning a new trick—how to present in front of a group. It took a lot of practice and hard work, but a year later, I presented a session that people said was interesting and helpful. I've been delivering conference presentations, webinars, and courses ever since. It feels great to share my knowledge and help others, and now I get more excited than nervous when I'm in front of a group. But I still hate calling strangers on the phone.

How to be happier by learning new tricks

I wanted to start the book by looking at learning new tricks, because you need to do that in order to apply the things you'll learn in all the other chapters. You can read stacks of books on happiness, but you'll only *become* happier if you actually use all that information to change your own life—and that means learning to do something new.

Find your "why"

Your first step is to determine which new skills or habits will add the most happiness to your life. You need to expect a substantial reward for your effort, or you won't stick with it. People often think they know what will make their lives better: making more money, losing weight, changing careers, or whatever. Ask yourself: *Why* would it make my life better? Keep asking yourself this question, using your previous answer as the starting point. For example:

I want to change careers.
Why?
Because I want a job where people appreciate me.
Why?
Because I need to know that what I do matters to people.
Why?
Because feeling like I'm making a difference in people's lives will make me happy.

No matter where your questions start, they should end with "it will make me happy." Then you know you've found the right new trick to learn. If the end result is anything other than more happiness (for example, if it just leads to impressing your peers), learning that new trick is not worth your time and effort.

Start now

Learning new tricks can help you become happier, but if you're stuck in old habits it can be uncomfortable to change your routine. As Duncan says, "The act of building new habits and skills will require some effort. You're going to have to use your brain when you don't want to. You'll have to unplug from autopilot. You'll need to surrender to being sucky at new skills for a little bit."

To avoid this discomfort, you might put off starting to learn your new tricks. It's all too easy to tell yourself you'll do it later because now is not a good time. Happiness expert Stephanie Staples says, "I just find so many people are waiting for a better time, a better space, better people around them, better something. *Now* is the time for you to be happy or healthy or more adventurous." Making your happiness a priority is essential because it gives you permission to start right away. Staples suggests, "Work harder on yourself than on anything else."

Make it rewarding

How can we take a more dog-like approach to learning the tricks that will make us happier? We can use our ingrained love of new things to generate enthusiasm for our pursuits, just like dogs do. Our brains notice new things more than things we see or do every day. Signing up for a new exercise class might make it easier to get into the exercise habit. Trying new recipes might make it more fun to cook healthy meals instead of ordering in. Or trying a new time management app might reduce your stress about having too much to do.

With dogs, it's important to reward the trick right away. There's nothing more effective than positive reinforcement—when they do what you want, good things happen. Do the same for yourself. Take a moment to celebrate every time you get something right. Did you apply for that dream job? Amazing! Did you buy vegetables instead of chips? Good for you! Pat yourself on the back, do a little happy dance, and remind yourself that you've taken one more step toward your goals and your happier life. Remember what we learned about dogs: the reward doesn't need to be a literal treat—it can be an opportunity to do something fun for a little while, praise for getting the trick right (including self-praise), or recognition from someone whose opinion you value.

This approach helps you feel good about your new tricks right away. You can't master a trick until you start practicing, but getting really good at it might seem like a distant or even impossible goal. Take it one step at a time. Even if you've only made a plan or set time aside in your schedule to work on your new trick, that's an important step. By celebrating every step, you focus on your progress, not on how far there is to go.

Of course, with dogs, sometimes you can't reward the trick right on the spot. For example, if they're learning to stay, you can't reward them while they're staying across the room. Instead, some people use "clicker training" to tell the dog they got it right. The trainer presses a clicker that makes a sound when the dog gets the trick right, and then gives the dog a treat when the trick is finished. The dog learns to associate that sound with knowing that a treat is coming soon. The positive reinforcement still works, even if the reward comes later.

That promise of delayed gratification can work for us too. You might not feel great while you're sweating at the gym first thing in the morning, but you soon learn that it will make you feel really good about yourself for the rest of the day, and you'll have more energy. The anticipation of that feeling becomes the trigger that gets you out of bed and into the gym.

Paws and reflect

- 🐾 To make any meaningful change in your life, including adding more happiness, you'll need to learn some new behaviors and habits.
- 🐾 The best way to learn new tricks is with repetition, consistency, and encouragement.
- 🐾 Identify your "why" to figure out which new tricks will add the most happiness to your life.
- 🐾 Don't wait for the "right time" to start something new. Start right away and give yourself time to become good at it.
- 🐾 Just because you've mastered a new trick in one context (when you're at home) doesn't mean you will automatically find it easy in other contexts (when you're having a night out or on vacation). Build up your new habits until they are easy to apply in every situation.
- 🐾 Reward yourself for getting things right (even partially right) instead of scolding yourself when you slip up. Associating positive feelings with your new trick will make you more likely to keep it up over the long run.

Photo credit: Patricia Prentice "Baloo"

2
Live in the moment

Pawsitive dogma

Be happy right now. Each new moment presents you with the possibility of happiness, and it's up to you to gratefully embrace it.

Note from Nuka

I'm usually paying attention to whatever is happening right in front of me. Anything I can smell, hear, see, touch, or (with a bit of luck) taste is important. Nothing else is really relevant, is it? I'm not going to sit around thinking about that rabbit I chased this morning but couldn't catch. And I'm definitely not worrying about when my next trip to the vet is coming up and what might be wrong with me.

Dogs mostly live in the moment. You should try it too. Instead, you always seem to be replaying stuff that already happened, even though it's over. Or worse, you're obsessed with stuff that hasn't even happened yet—and might never happen. All that "what if" is so distracting. Half the time, I bet you don't even notice what's going on around you. Life is full of good stuff if you pay attention. Remember to enjoy it!

What the dog experts say

For dogs, paying attention to exactly what is happening started out as a matter of survival: Are they somewhere safe? Are they too hot or cold? Are there any immediate threats? Is there something to eat? When their survival wasn't under threat, paying attention could maximize their happiness: Is there something interesting to smell? Is there a fun game to join? Dogs have little to gain from pondering the past or the future. And because they have little to gain from such pondering, their brains aren't wired for it.

According to dog behavior specialist Ian Dunbar, "Humans clog up vital brain power with hypothetical constructions, theoretical conundrums, moot points, obtuse fallacies and heuristic paradoxes. Dogs excel at analyzing and enjoying the moment by savoring every single ounce of pure pleasure of the present."

That's not to say that dogs have no understanding of time. You've probably noticed they seem to know when it's their usual time to have dinner or go for a walk. They also seem tuned in to when a member of their human family usually comes home from work or school. So time does have meaning to dogs, they just don't project their thoughts backward or forward very far. They concern themselves with the situation at hand—what's happening or what *should* be happening.

Anthrozoologist John Bradshaw says, "One notable difference between dogs' emotional lives and our own is that their sense of time is much less sophisticated. Their ability to think back into their past, to mull over what has happened—even quite recently—and make sense of it, seems almost nonexistent." He says that dogs don't reflect on their past actions to try to figure out why they did those things and what they might have done differently, like we do. If your dog gets sprayed while chasing a skunk, they likely aren't sitting at home later, thinking about how they could have avoided the awful stink if they'd only left that skunk alone. That connection between past events and current results is not very strong.

Dogs anticipate things that are going to happen in the immediate future, but not very far ahead. For example, when they see you put a suitcase next to the door, they may know from experience that you're going to leave for a long time. They may start acting anxious at this point, but only once the evidence is in front of them. They won't mope around for weeks, speculating that you might go on a trip soon.

In other words, dogs don't let things in the past or future—things they can't currently control—get in the way of enjoying the moment.

Nuka had a severe autoimmune reaction of some kind (we still don't know what triggered it, but we noticed she was lethargic and had some strange dark spots on the undersides of her ears). The platelet count in her blood fell dangerously low. That meant she was in serious danger of bleeding to death if she got a cut, and it also meant her blood wasn't able to deliver nutrients and oxygen around her body like it should. We had to put her on powerful steroids and have her blood taken every week for a few months to monitor her recovery. It was quite an ordeal for her. But despite getting taken to the vet and having blood drawn over and over again, every time we took her out to the car her tail would wag and she would happily jump in. It was as though she kept thinking, "This time I bet we're going to the beach!" It wasn't until she arrived at the vet's office that she acted scared or anxious. Her ability to keep a positive attitude about car trips was kind of amazing, and she still gets excited to jump in the car because, just often enough, we go to the beach.

What the happiness experts say

Just how bad are humans at living in the moment? According to a 2010 study from Harvard University, most people spend only about 50% of their time in the present moment. So half of the time, you're mentally somewhere else, thinking about the past or the future, wondering what's going on in another place, or worrying about things that aren't currently happening.

Happiness expert Stephanie Staples says that, as a result, we lose our time. "I think what happens is your time evaporates. So many people want more time in their day. The most precious commodity is time. But when we're at work, we're thinking about home and when we're at home, we're thinking about work—wherever we are, we're thinking about somewhere else." Before long, the day is over and you feel like you didn't do anything interesting or fun. Why not? What were you so busy with that you couldn't enjoy your day? Chances are, you spent a lot of it not even noticing the good things that were right in front of you.

Social welfare expert Katherine Compitus thinks we're not just missing out on things, we're also putting a huge burden on ourselves. "We're often focused on the things that are out of our control—and most things are out of our control. Once we accept that, we no longer have the responsibility to control other people, to control the weather, to control our environment. We should try to stay away from those responsibilities because they're not real, they're theoretical constructs. When we look at the world as it is, instead of how we wish it was, it releases that burden and we make more peace with ourselves."

She often advises her clients to be aware that they are all right in that moment, that they are safe and not under threat. For people who are experiencing a lot of anxiety or fixated on past trauma, it can be easy to forget that the stressful events are over and they're free to enjoy themselves in the moment. When you find yourself thinking about something bad that happened at work, or something coming up that you're nervous about, it's important to stop and remember that at this very moment, you are perfectly fine and nothing bad is happening. You are free to be happy.

Letting go of things you can't control is hard, but it's the only way you can truly live in the moment. If you're worried about something, ask yourself whether you can do anything about it right now. If you can, then it may be worth devoting your time to. If not, you are simply wasting your time, so try to push those thoughts aside and bring yourself back to what you can do now.

I walk my dogs early in the morning, as the sun is just rising. Often, I catch myself thinking about the work that's waiting for me at home, the emails I need to answer, and any number of other things I can't do anything about while I'm on the walk. Thankfully, one of our walking routes passes through a clifftop park at the edge of Lake Ontario. If the timing is right, I get to see the sunrise over the lake, which can be breathtakingly beautiful. The sunrise is usually behind me, so I need to intentionally stop and turn around to enjoy the moment. After years of sunrises, I still treasure those moments every single time. I love seeing the pink light glowing on the undersides of the clouds and the colors reflected on the rippling surface of the lake, but the moment is fleeting and easy to miss. Each time, I am reminded that there is great beauty in the world if we simply remember to stop and notice it.

How to be happier by living in the moment

There's little doubt that we can enjoy life more if we live in the moment, but making it happen takes effort. As I said in "Learn new tricks," you'll need to form new habits and patterns and leave some of your old ones behind.

Here are a few simple approaches you can take to start living in the moment more often:

1. Mindfulness
2. Meditation
3. Savoring

I'll go through these one by one. It could be that only one of them will work for you—or maybe you'll adopt two or even all three. Use what works best for you. Every change you embrace is an opportunity to be happier.

Mindfulness

You might be tired of hearing about mindfulness—it has become a real buzzword, and people use it to mean all kinds of different things. In the end, mindfulness just means paying attention to what you're doing.

Start with something simple you do every day. Maybe it's walking to the bus stop or picking up your kids from school. Target that activity and observe what's around you, how you feel, and what you hear and smell as well as what you see. How does the sun feel? Can you hear the breeze blowing through the leaves of the trees? Are there birds chirping? Can you see where they are? How does your body feel today? Is anything tensed up that you could relax? Your shoulders? Your jaw? If you catch yourself thinking about other things, stop and redirect your mind to what you're doing.

Once you've practiced doing this during one activity, start trying to do it with more and more: eating meals, exercising, driving, shopping. Whenever you find your mind wandering ahead to your to-do list or replaying things that happened in the past, try to bring yourself back to the moment and find things to enjoy, appreciate, and focus on. Your dog is happy to walk around the same block every day because it's always a slightly different experience. So are your everyday experiences—if you take time to notice the details.

Meditation

There is a ton of research on the benefits of meditation. It has been found to give you better control of your emotions, more self-awareness, more positive emotions (and fewer negative ones), improved memory, more flexible thinking, and a stronger immune system. It can also reduce depression and anxiety, physical illness, and time spent dwelling on negative thoughts.

Meditation used to be associated with yoga retreats and Buddhist monks, but these days there are all kinds of books, videos, and apps available, all designed to help you practice calming your mind. The goal of meditation is to quiet the constant chatter inside your head and let you simply be in the moment. This can take a while to get used to, so don't expect to have a transformative experience the first time you try it. But for many people, meditation resets their brains to neutral or positive instead of constantly ramping up the stress, and it helps them control their stress better throughout the day.

If you've never practiced meditation before, you might need to try a few different approaches before you find something that works for you. But most people who get into a regular habit of meditation feel it makes a big difference in how they handle stress and lets them enjoy their lives more.

If sitting still is really not your thing, a repetitive activity that focuses your mind on your breath and body can be a pretty good substitute for meditation. I actually find that swimming laps puts me in a meditation-like state. Obviously, I need to focus on my breath when I swim to avoid breathing the water in. I have to be constantly aware of my body position and my movements so that my rhythm is steady, and by counting laps I can stop my mind from wandering off in other directions. If you're not a swimmer, walking or running can offer the same opportunity to focus. But if you're listening to your favorite tunes or saying hello to everyone you pass (or their dogs), you aren't meditating.

Savoring

Savoring is closely linked to gratitude, a practice that can significantly increase happiness. When you focus on a pleasant experience and draw as much pleasure from it as possible, it actually helps to implant that pleasant feeling in your brain and keep it there longer. Pleasure is often fleeting, and while you might spend endless hours replaying the unpleasant things that happened during your day, chances are you don't reflect as much on the good things, because you didn't give them your full attention in the moment.

Positive psychology expert Bridget Grenville-Cleave suggests five steps to help you savor an experience. An easy way to try this out is with a food you really enjoy. Let's take eating chocolate as a simple example:

1. *Slow down.* Don't just chew and swallow. Take small bites and let the chocolate melt in your mouth for a few seconds. Stop and reflect between each bite. Put the chocolate down between bites so you're forced to eat more slowly.

2. *Pay attention to what you are doing.* Don't do anything else while you're eating. If you're busy watching a video or putting away groceries, you aren't paying enough attention to the experience of eating.

3. *Use all your senses.* Remember to taste the chocolate. It seems obvious, but you may go into autopilot and find you've suddenly finished eating it without event noticing how it tasted. And add your senses of smell and touch. Hear and feel the snap of the chocolate when you take a bite. Appreciate the change in texture as it coats your mouth.

4. *Stretch out the experience.* Pause between bites. Stop and appreciate how good this tastes and how it affects your mood. Think about the good things you associate with chocolate.

5. *Reflect on your enjoyment.* Take a moment to appreciate how fortunate you are to be eating this delicious chocolate today. In fact, you should be grateful you live in a world with chocolate! Be aware that you've had a special treat. Dwell on the flavor lingering in your mouth. Take note of the pleasure and hold on to it for a few moments.

Savoring positive experiences as they happen forms the basis of psychologist and positive neuroplasticity expert Rick Hanson's book, *Hardwiring Happiness*. According to Hanson, by keeping positive experiences front of mind for just 20 seconds or so before you move on, you can actually change the connections in your brain to make you feel happier in general. He calls this type of savoring "taking in the good" and says, "You can build up both your capacity to *be* satisfied and your sense of *feeling* satisfied by regularly taking in pleasure, gratitude and gladness, positive emotion, accomplishment and agency, enthusiasm, the fullness of this moment, and contentment."

Most of us experience good things many, many times every day, but we don't consider them significant enough to pay attention to them. While you've probably heard "don't sweat the small stuff," perhaps you haven't often heard the flip side: take pleasure in the small stuff.

Dogs enjoy every belly rub, meal, walk, and opportunity to play. If we look at our lives as a string of mostly positive events and enjoy them as they unfold, we set ourselves up for greater happiness.

Paws and reflect

- People are generally bad at living in the moment. We spend half our time either replaying past events or worrying about the future.

- We miss a lot of opportunities to have positive thoughts and experiences because we aren't appreciating what's happening right now.

- When you are thinking about things you can't do anything about at the moment, make yourself let go of those thoughts and refocus your attention on the present.

- Practice mindfulness to take in your experiences more fully. Make a point of bringing yourself back to the present moment when your mind wanders.

- Try using meditation or similar practices to learn how to calm the mental noise that keeps you preoccupied.

- Savor every positive feeling fully, using all your senses, and keep your focus on each good feeling for longer so it becomes imprinted on your mind.

Photo credit: Alexa for Pixabay

3
Wag your tail

Pawsitive dogma

Share your joy with all the world by wagging your tail. Why hide your happiness when you can spread it to everyone?

Message from Marlowe

Look, it's not complicated. If I'm happy I wag my tail to let you know. Sure, we can drill down into details. There's the laid back "Hey, I see you're looking at me" wag, the faster "time for a walk" wag, and the "Yay! You're finally home from your trip" swinging around in circles like a helicopter wag.

I have to say, it's very handy having a tail so I can tell you how I feel. You humans sometimes forget to show your feelings, especially your happy feelings. Sure, you celebrate big stuff like getting a new job or winning a competition, but why don't you celebrate the little stuff, like a good hair day, a task you got done, or a yummy meal? When you wag your tail for every good thing that happens, you remind yourself (and everyone around you) to be happy.

What the dog experts say

Dogs wag their tails as a form of communication—with other dogs and with people. You might think a dog's tail wags whenever they're happy, but they only do it when there's someone around to see it. Dogs don't wag their tails at their toys or at the bone they're enjoying. Dog behavior expert Stanley Coren says, "A dog reserves tail wagging for things that are alive. In some ways, tail wagging serves the same communication functions as a human smile, a polite greeting, or a nod of recognition."

In fact, tails are an important communication tool for dogs. Researchers studying wolf behavior noticed at least 13 tail postures with different meanings. Dogs have much of the same vocabulary. A tail hung low or tucked between a dog's legs is a sign of depression or fear. A tail held high, straight, and puffed out (or even vibrating) is signaling aggression or dominance. So when a tail is wagging with a big swoosh, it's a good indication that the dog is relaxed and comfortable, and the intensity of the wagging mirrors the intensity of the dog's joy or excitement.

Expressing their state of mind is important for dogs, especially when they're around other dogs. Poor communication skills can lead to conflict. Dogs with very short tails (because some people have their dog's tail "docked," or cut short according to breed standards) tend to get into more fights with other dogs. It may be difficult for them to show other dogs that their intentions are friendly.

Does the same thing happen when people fail to communicate their pleasure or friendliness? If you share your little moments of happiness, not only do you make yourself feel better, you help those around you to feel better and more comfortable with you. When a dog sees you and starts wagging their tail, doesn't it make you feel good that they're happy to see you? You have that power too.

> Marlowe and Nuka get dinner around the same time every day. They've had thousands of dinners over the years, and yet they still act delighted every time they know it's coming. Nuka, in particular, does this adorable little happy dance where she wags her tail, taps her feet, and shifts her weight back and forth, as if she can barely contain her excitement. I remember watching Snoopy on TV in cartoon specials when I was a kid, doing his famous "suppertime dance." I thought it was fun and silly, but when we adopted Nuka I realized it wasn't much of an exaggeration. If dinner makes you happy, it's worth celebrating every day.

What the happiness experts say

Why bother celebrating the little stuff that happens every day? It turns out, all those little positive moments in your day can really add up. And you need them to add up because, as I mentioned in the introduction, your brain has a negativity bias—you have way more negative thoughts every day than positive thoughts, and you remember them more. Positive neuroplasticity expert Rick Hanson likes to say, "The mind is like Velcro for negative experiences and like Teflon for positive experiences." The negatives stick around and the positives slip away. As a result of this bias, you need to ramp up the number of positive thoughts you have every day if you want to be happier.

According to positive psychology expert Bridget Grenville-Cleave, researchers have discovered that the *frequency* of positive thoughts is more important than their *intensity* when it comes to making you happy. She also has some suggestions for how you can increase those positive thoughts by celebrating more often. She notes how we all celebrate small things when we're children but seem to lose that ability as we grow up: "Remember how excited, enthusiastic and expressive you were as a child when good things happened? Next time you feel really good about something, why not throw caution to the wind and dance for joy, punch the air or whoop with delight? It may not feel like you to start with, but with a little practice you can recapture some of the natural ebullience that you had as a child. There is evidence that expressing your positive feelings externally can intensify them, so why not give it a go?" Think about how you reacted as a child when someone handed you an ice cream cone.

Most likely, your face lit up, and maybe you shouted, "Yessss! Ice cream!" When was the last time you openly celebrated the small stuff like that?

This is definitely one area where dogs have a lot to teach us. Happiness coach Kim Strobel has been rescuing homeless dogs for years. She says, "I feel like dogs appreciate every single, tiny, wonderful thing around them. Our brains have so much information coming at us that we're not paying attention to the goodness unless we train our brains to pay attention. Dogs, unlike humans at times, are so appreciative of the tiniest little thing. We take all of those things for granted." She encourages people not only to notice the little things that make their day better but to express gratitude for them too.

Celebrating our own small wins is helpful, but happiness expert Stephanie Staples suggests we should also get our friends and loved ones to join the celebration. External validation can make a small celebration feel like a bigger deal. She says, "It is nice to get that pat on the back from somebody else. So what's wrong with asking for what you need? Your dogs do that, right? When they're not getting enough attention, they come up and rub against you and they let you know what they need. It would be cool if we could all do that. And if we gave each other permission to do that." When something good happens, tell people about it. Their congratulations will make you feel even better, and maybe it will make their day better too.

I went from running in my first 10K race to being barely able to move in less than a year, thanks to a disc injury in my lower back around five years ago. My recovery was so slow and painful that I wasn't sure I'd ever be able to run again. When I started to feel a bit stronger, I began jogging a little on my treadmill. I'd do just a few minutes of running with walking intervals in between, but after fearing I would never run again, it felt like a big win to even start this journey. Sometimes I do a bit too much and end up having to stop completely for a while, but I keep trying again when I feel up to it. And every time I run a little more than last time, I consider it a big win and tell my husband about my amazing accomplishment. Even if I never run 10K again, I'm a winner every time I get off that treadmill without causing a relapse of my back injury, and I try to never forget it.

How to be happier by wagging your tail

Maybe this would be easier if we actually had tails to wag, but people do have the capacity to express joy in many ways. It begins, of course, with noticing the good things you can celebrate every day. If you've started living in the moment, you're halfway there already.

Reflect on the good stuff

One way to incorporate more celebration into your life is to look back at the end of each day and think about the things that went well. What did you accomplish? Did you try anything new? Did you do something better than the last time you tried it? Did you help someone? Write it all down in a journal you can look back at when you're feeling down, or put small slips of paper with your accomplishments in a "win jar" that you open at the end of the year.

Gathering up your celebration material once a day is a good way to start getting into the habit of noticing what's going well. But it's even more powerful to celebrate things as soon as they happen. Get used to wagging that tail! If you do nothing else, smile to yourself about it. The simple act of smiling will help your mood stay positive for longer. Hold the positive mood at the front of your mind for a moment and let it sink in.

Count the small wins

Try not to filter out anything as not "important" enough to celebrate. It's easy to talk yourself out of your positive feelings by deciding your experiences aren't worthy of celebration. Everything is worthy—remember, you need to have *a lot* of positive thoughts each day to counteract your negativity bias. Even things you do every single day are worth celebrating. Did you bring your lunch to work instead of buying it? Did you neatly braid your child's hair? Did you stand up for yourself at work? Did you make an appointment you were putting off? Did you eat some fresh fruits or vegetables? These are all things worth celebrating. You're a big winner!

Celebrate without working for it

You can also celebrate things that happened with no actual effort on your part. Just because you didn't work for it doesn't mean it's not worth adding to your growing number of positive thoughts. You can celebrate the nice weather, the comforting smell of buttered toast, the fact that fresh strawberries are in season, a new season of a TV show you like, the cozy feeling when you snuggle into your bed, or anything that makes your day a little better.

You can even celebrate other people's good stuff. If your partner, colleague, or friend has something to celebrate, join in the fun and make a fuss. Let their positive mood become your positive mood. If your child did well on a test, get excited about it and talk to them about how it makes them feel. If your friend got a raise or a promotion, get together and mark the occasion.

Not only are you adding to your number of positive thoughts, you're forming a stronger emotional bond with your friends, family, and colleagues.

Amplify your positive thoughts

Intensify your positive thoughts with positive self-talk. You can do this inside your head, or you can do it in writing or out loud. For instance, you can write "Great presentation today!" on a sticky note and stick it to your wall or monitor. Keep it up there all day to remind yourself how well it went. When you make it through your entire workout or yoga routine, congratulate yourself on a job well done.

Want an extra happiness boost? Celebrate your positive experiences at the time, then celebrate again with your dog when you get home. Tell them your good news in your most excited voice, so they know how amazing it is. Dogs are always ready to celebrate with you, even if they have no idea why!

You can also send a message to a friend or loved one to tell them about something good that just happened. It may not seem like a big enough event to bother them with, but sharing your positive experiences makes them feel more important and makes you feel happier about them. You can get your main supporters ready for this by telling them you'll be sending good news messages regularly. Let them know that a simple happy face from them, or a "good for you" response, would really be appreciated. It will take only a couple of seconds of their time, and you can offer to do the same thing for them in exchange.

Wagging your tail isn't about boasting or making anyone else feel bad in comparison. It's simply about recognizing the good things in your life and truly appreciating them like dogs do, every single time they happen. Give yourself the opportunity to experience more positive thoughts by expressing joy, excitement, and gratitude as often as possible.

Paws and reflect

- When you openly show people your happiness, it makes them feel happier too. A good mood is contagious.
- You need to have a large number of positive thoughts to counteract your brain's negativity bias, so it's important to take note of all the positive things that happen each day.
- Thinking about your positive experiences from throughout the day—and even writing them down in a journal or adding them to a "win jar"—can help reinforce how much happiness you actually experience each day.
- Remember that every good thing is worth celebrating, even if it seems insignificant at the time.
- You can celebrate good things you didn't work for (like a nice day) and good things that happen to people around you. You don't need to put effort into something to have positive feelings about it.

🐾 Share your good experiences to get an extra boost of happiness from the positive reactions of friends, colleagues, and family—and your dog.

Photo credit: Christiel Sagniez for Pixabay

4
Never stop playing

Pawsitive dogma

Playing is an expression of pure happiness because it lets you enjoy things just for the sake of enjoying them.

Note from Nuka

Why would I ever want to stop playing? First of all, it's great for my social life. I get to hang out with my people or my dog friends. It's good for my physical fitness and also for my brain, because I have to solve problems and figure stuff out on the fly. But mostly, it's just so much fun!

My people like playing with me, but they don't play much without me. They seem to think it's not a good use of their time, like they have more important things they should be doing. I don't know about that. Playing seems *pretty important to me, especially since it makes them so happy! What could be more important than that? You should definitely play more if you want to be happier. And you should definitely play more with me!*

What the dog experts say

Just like human children play a lot more than adults, puppies play a lot more than most adult dogs. There's a good reason for them to spend so much time playing. Puppies play to learn about communicating with other dogs, develop physical coordination, and learn bite inhibition (play biting without hurting each other). It's like practice for becoming a dog. And because we usually play with our puppies, it also teaches them how to interact with humans, and how that's different from interacting with dogs. Dog behavior expert Ian Dunbar says, "It is vital that puppies grow up in an enriched social and physical environment that offers adequate opportunity to play with toys, to play with each other, to play with dogs of different ages, and to play with people."

One of the important things dogs learn is how to signal that they are playing. This often involves the "play bow," where the dog's front legs are on the ground and their bum is up in the air. It's the "let's play" signal that tells other dogs (and us) when a game is about to begin, or when it can start again after a break. Dog behavior expert Alexandra Horowitz has extensively studied dogs at play. She says, "If you fail to signal before biting, jumping on, hip-slamming, and standing over your playmate, you are not in fact playing; you are assaulting him. A bout wherein only one participant thinks it's play is no longer playful. Without the

4. NEVER STOP PLAYING   53

play signal, a bite is a bite, worthy of rancor or retribution. With it, a bite is just part of the game."

This is an incredibly important thing to learn, especially for wild canines. Marc Bekoff is a professor of evolutionary biology and he says that, just like dogs, coyotes have rules of social interaction that help them cooperate. Coyotes that don't learn the rules, or don't play by the rules, are kicked out of the group and must survive on their own. Not learning how to get along with others can turn into a death sentence in the wild. This shows that coyotes use a kind of morality—those who break the rules of the community are punished by being sent away. Morality is a characteristic that was long thought to be exclusively human, but it seems like we're finding more and more evidence of it in other social species.

It's clear that puppies need to play so they can learn all these rules, but why do adult dogs keep playing? Part of it is because they can—they have the luxury of being fed and sheltered by people, and that leaves them with a lot of spare time. But it's also because we've bred them over time to stay more like puppies. This is called "neoteny." Things like floppy ears, short snouts, and large "puppy dog" eyes are all puppy-like features that humans have decided we like. We choose to breed dogs who are friendly and playful, so we have genetically selected them to keep playing throughout life.

Dogs like playing so much that they'll make sure they don't win too fast and end the game early. For example, if you've ever played tug-of-war with a large dog, it's clear the dog's jaws are much stronger than your grip. Often, the dog will pull just hard enough to challenge you but not rip the toy out of your hands.

Dogs also restrain their play with other dogs. A big dog will play lying down or on their back to let a smaller dog play safely with them. For dogs, playing is more important than winning.

Playing is obviously a priority for dogs, and research has shown it does make them happy (as if you couldn't tell just by watching). Anthrozoologist John Bradshaw says, "Play and happiness seem inextricably linked in dogs, consistent with the idea that they are wolves that never grew up. When a dog catches sight of a favorite toy and starts playing with it spontaneously, that impromptu activity will have been generated by the feeling of happiness that the dog recalls from the last time it played with that toy."

> Marlowe's and Nuka's faces always light up with excitement as soon as we arrive at the dog park. The open space itself is glorious, and if we arrive first they take off at full tilt, just enjoying the freedom and the rush of running far and fast. But when other dogs are there, Marlowe's favorite game has always been chase. He'll wait for another dog to take off and be in hot pursuit. He has never liked being chased, just chasing. Once he grew out of puppyhood, Marlowe lost most of his interest in toys. But he has never grown out of a good chase—it's his favorite kind of play.

What the happiness experts say

When children play, it serves a lot of the same purposes as puppy play does (including the lesson about not biting other kids). They learn how to interact with others, follow rules, take turns, and cooperate. They also practice grown-up skills in a safe way. They might play at running a household and being parents, being doctors and taking care of patients, being teachers for their stuffies, engineering structures out of blocks, or whatever grown-up activities they want to try out. They also learn physical coordination and mental problem-solving. Playing is serious business for kids.

Eventually, though, you were probably told to stop spending so much time playing and get down to the serious business of studying, learning skills, and then working. When adults (or even older children) act playful, they're often accused of "wasting time" and told to get back to work.

Playing is not wasted time—it's important for stretching your brain in a different direction. When you take a break from a difficult task or problem and do something fun for a while, the solution often comes to you much faster. You become more innovative and creative. Playing allows you to look at things in an open, unstructured way, with more possibilities and fewer rules.

Happiness coach Kim Strobel is a big supporter of lifelong play. She says, "Play literally changes the brain. When you can get your brain to be positive rather than negative, neutral, or stressed, we see a 31% increase in productivity levels, and we see that you're 10 times more engaged in what you're doing. You're three times more creative. Something as simple as play really does get your brain bouncing back."

Stuart Brown, founder of the National Institute for Play, says that when you continue to play throughout your life, your brain continues to make new connections and stay healthy. "The brain can keep developing long after we leave adolescence and play promotes that growth. We are designed to be lifelong players, built to benefit from play at any age." As you age, playing becomes even more important. Physical play, as well as doing puzzles and playing mentally challenging games, helps prevent dementia and other cognitive issues in older people.

Brown also says that the idea of play being the enemy of work and vice versa is wrong. We need both. "What I have found is that neither one can thrive without the other. We need the newness of play, its sense of flow, and being in the moment. We also need the purpose of work, the economic stability that it offers, the sense that we are doing service for others, that we are needed and integrated into our world." We need to find the right balance between work and play to be truly happy.

In addition to opening up your mind to creativity and positivity, playing can make you feel young again. Remember how happy and free you felt when you played as a child? Playing can help relieve the stress of adult life and also help you rediscover what makes you happiest. On the other hand, people who have no opportunities to play tend to lose their sense of optimism and find it difficult to experience lasting pleasure.

Social welfare expert Katherine Compitus thinks play is a great way for her clients to get in touch with their feelings and their needs. "I don't know where we got this message that we shouldn't be playing," she says. "Playing does a lot for us.

Not only do we feel good and recharged, we oftentimes get in touch with our younger self. We're so busy all the time—worried about what everybody else thinks and expects and wants—that we ignore ourselves. When we can turn around and be more connected to ourselves, it's a way to enjoy life."

Brown concludes that playing is "critical not only to being happy, but also to sustaining social relationships and being a creative, innovative person. But in the end the most significant aspect of play is that it allows us to express our joy and connect most deeply with the best in ourselves, and in others."

> While I was researching this book, I realized that my workdays were dragging. (Not while I was researching, which I enjoyed, but while I was doing other work.) I started thinking about how to put myself in a more positive mood at the beginning of the day. After all, what's the point of researching happiness if you're not going to test it out on yourself? Every morning before I sat down at my desk, I'd put on a couple of songs that I love and do a little dancing. I'm not a good dancer, but I used to like going out to clubs in my 20s and dancing with friends. I miss that, although I'd never be able to stay awake late enough now! So adding some boogie back into my life helps put me in a good mood and energizes me as I start my day.

How to be happier by playing

The connection between play and feeling happy is pretty obvious. Playing makes you happy because you choose the types of play that make you feel good—why else would you bother? Because of this connection, paying more attention to *how* you like to play often reveals your strengths and your passions, and it may even help you choose a more fulfilling career, or at least a hobby that will make you happier.

The big trick is finding ways to introduce more play into your life after you've become used to not playing. There are many ways to go about this, but let's look at some of the easiest ways to make your life more playful.

Embrace a playful attitude

Play doesn't have to be a separate event that you set aside time for. Happiness expert Stephanie Staples claims, "You can add playfulness to just about everything." Whether you're trying to score a three-pointer by lobbing your empty can into the recycling bin, dancing to the oldies in the supermarket aisle, or texting emojis to a colleague during a boring online meeting, you can find ways to make your day more playful.

At first, you might feel self-conscious about acting playful. The fear of not being taken seriously can deter you from throwing yourself into playful behavior. But most of the time (unless something particularly serious is happening) everyone around you will appreciate your positive mood, and it will help them feel happier too. Which colleagues do you prefer spending time with: the ones who stare at their monitors all day and never say anything that isn't work-related, or the ones who tell you about the funny thing that happened to them over lunch or send you cute puppy videos? Work can be both productive and playful, as long as you know when it's appropriate to be goofy and when to put the fun on hold for a bit.

Home life is much the same. Maybe you've seen the famous scene in the movie *The Big Chill*, where a group of friends are dancing and singing while they wash the dishes. Whatever you're doing, try to have a little more fun while you do it.

Find your play style

Not everyone has the same definition of "play." Some people think riding their bike for five hours to another city is a fun way to spend the day; others think that's some kind of torture. Some people love to go to big concerts; others can't stand being in a crowd.

Finding your ideal play style is usually automatic. You naturally gravitate toward things that are fun for you. But it is interesting to intentionally think about what makes you feel like you're having a good time. Brown's research on play led him to define eight different play personalities:

- The Joker, who likes to goof around and play practical jokes
- The Kinesthete, who needs to be in motion in order to think
- The Explorer, who yearns for either physical or mental exploration

- The Competitor, who enjoys keeping score and trying to win
- The Director, who enjoys planning and executing activities and is always organizing things
- The Collector, who enjoys collecting and categorizing things and ticking stuff off their bucket list
- The Artist/Creator, who enjoys art, crafts, cooking, or tinkering
- The Storyteller, who enjoys writing or creating a narrative to motivate their activities

Do one or more of those play personalities sound like you? You may be strongly tied to one, or you may be a combination of several of them. I'm an Explorer-Director-Storyteller. If you have trouble figuring out what your play style is, try to think back to your favorite things to do when you were a child. Chances are, they reflect your natural play style and you would still enjoy those kinds of things. If you loved dance classes, you are probably a Kinesthete. If you had Pokémon or stickers all carefully organized in albums, or comic books kept in plastic sleeves, you are likely a Collector.

Thinking about your play personality can help you choose activities that will make you happy. If you're an Explorer, going on a spontaneous road trip might be your ideal play experience. If you're a Competitor, perhaps joining a team or league of some kind would give you a chance to compete regularly and move up the rankings. Whatever you enjoy, try to focus your playtime on the things that make you feel happiest.

Play with others

If you have young children or pets, you have built-in playmates available. Just like big dogs adapt to make it more fun to play with smaller dogs, you can adapt to play with children and pets by getting down to their level, not throwing the ball too hard, or making whatever adjustments are needed. The obvious joy you see when children or pets are playing is contagious, and you can lift your mood just by participating in their fun activities. Brown visits his local dog park regularly with his rescue dog Cookie, and he finds that "the contagion of play when I experience it full on in dog-dog play has a mood and body-altering effect just from watching it!"

Even if you don't have your own kids or pets, you can get the same benefit by coaching a sports team, pet sitting, babysitting your relatives' children, walking in dog-friendly parks, or teaching something you enjoy.

If you have friends who enjoy the same activities that you do, make a point of doing them together more often. Those activities may have been what sparked your friendship in the first place, but sometimes, as lives change, things you used to do regularly happen less and less often. Pick up some of your old activities, or try something new together.

If the people you know aren't into the same games or activities as you, seek out groups or organizations that bring together like-minded strangers for fun. Sports leagues, book clubs, dance classes, and hiking clubs are just a few examples. Online gaming has opened up opportunities for more people to find "playmates" outside their circle of friends, without even leaving home.

Include passive play

Some people's ideal type of play doesn't match what we usually think of as playing. You can play without involving anyone else, and some people consider this their favorite way to relax. Introverts, for example, might find it draining to join a club or a team. If your idea of a perfect weekend is to stay at home reading books or binging a new series, that counts as playing too.

Going to movies, plays, live music events, and night clubs may not strictly sound like playing either, but it is. Even listening to your favorite music at home is a form of play—and if it makes you happier, dance like nobody's watching.

There are endless ways to include more play in your life, and all of them will help you increase your feelings of happiness and satisfaction. Dogs don't just squeeze in play when there's nothing else they should be doing—it's an important part of their routine. Prioritize play as much as you do eating, sleeping, and exercising—it's just as essential.

Paws and reflect

- 🐾 Time spent playing is not "wasted." It boosts your mood, makes you more productive, and can help you solve complex problems.

- 🐾 Playing (both physical and mental games) keeps your brain healthy and helps form new neural connections as you get older.

- 🐾 You can incorporate a playful attitude into most things you do. Playing doesn't need to happen at specific times.

- 🐾 Not everyone enjoys the same type of play. Find your ideal play style, and use it to choose activities that will give you the most happiness.

- 🐾 Spend time with people (or dogs) who enjoy the same activities you do. Make play a priority by scheduling time to do those things together.

- 🐾 Playing can include passive activities like listening to music, watching TV or movies, and reading books. Any mental escape can refresh your mind and put you in a more positive mood.

Photo credit: Steve Lancaster for Pixabay

5
Find your pack

Pawsitive dogma

Everything good is better when you share it with someone. Everything bad is less bad when you have someone to help you through it.

Message from Marlowe

Being alone is pretty much my least favorite thing. I mean, why would you want to be anywhere without me? I don't want to be without you! The dogsitter is pretty cool, but I'm happiest when my pack is around. That's my human family as well as Nuka and a few other dogs I like to hang out with. But you gotta earn a place in my pack—space is limited!

People need a pack too. Maybe not a big one, but at least a few other people they can talk to about stuff. Humans are like dogs that way—you aren't made to be alone all the time.

What the dog experts say

Packs are one of the most misunderstood aspects of canine life. That's because early canine researchers studied wolves in captivity and made assumptions based on their observations. But wolves in captivity aren't in natural packs, so they get into a lot more conflicts and power struggles than a wild wolf pack. A wild pack is usually just an extended family, with the "alpha" male and female being the heads of the family. Wolves cooperate when they hunt, and they all help to raise the pups. Sure, they have disagreements (like all families), but the myth of the aggressive alpha wolf and the constant battle for dominance among pack members has largely been debunked.

Dogs have branched off significantly from wolves anyway, so making assumptions about dogs' social groups based on wolf behavior can lead to misguided advice, like pinning your dog to the ground in an "alpha roll" to show them who's boss. Most dog trainers will confirm that positive reinforcement works better and creates a healthier relationship between dogs and their human family than trying to dominate them.

Because dogs have evolved alongside humans for so long, they have made the very unusual adaptation of bonding with us like family, or pack members. Anthrozoologist John Bradshaw says the change in dogs' brains may have been a result of domestication, or perhaps a certain (now extinct) line of wolves had this capacity already, and those were the wolves who chose to live with us and eventually evolved into dogs. A young puppy learns who their pack is during a crucial socialization period early in life, and a special space in their brain is reserved for those important pack members. Bradshaw says, "The evidence suggests that a dog born in a human household develops two such spaces, one for dogs and one for humans."

Dog behavior expert Stanley Coren says this ability makes dogs uniquely suited to be our companions. "Dogs have been socialized to two different species. They consider themselves to be part of a human pack as well as part of a canine pack. Since their genetics tell them they are part of a group, they will seek out our comfort as well as the comfort of other dogs."

Dog guardians often wonder whether their dog can really "love" them. Coren says that dogs' brains react to the people they're closest to much like human brains do. "Dogs even have the hormone oxytocin, which in humans is involved with love and affection for others. Given that dogs and people have the same neurology and chemistry, it seems reasonable to suggest that dogs also have emotions similar to ours." In other words, your dog does love you.

Dogs have been known to travel vast distances to reunite with their human families after getting lost. And social media is practically bursting with videos of overjoyed dogs being reunited with family members who have been absent for a long time, perhaps serving in the armed forces or recovering from an illness in hospital. Clearly, dogs hold us in their hearts just like we hold them in ours.

> When we adopted Marlowe, he was around five months old. Marlowe was the last of his litter to be adopted; he'd been with his foster family for almost four months during a critical time when he was learning who his pack was. When he was dropped off at our house, he was clearly waiting for his "mom" to come back and get him. He was not very playful, looked out the window a lot, and refused to go for walks (probably so he wouldn't miss her return). It took a little while for him to start accepting us as his new pack, but he did adjust and grow very attached to us before long. Just a few weeks later, while we were out for a walk, a neighbor said to me, "That dog really loves you. I can see it in the way he looks at you."

What the happiness experts say

Humans are one of a few species that are considered "super social." That means we have social connections throughout our lives, outside our immediate family group. We have built societies where we depend on various people taking on different roles, rather than having the skills within our household or clan to do everything we need to survive. That makes interacting with others more important for us than it is for most other species. Our survival depends on getting along with each other. As a result, our brains are wired for social interaction. Without it, we break down both emotionally and physically. We were not made to be hermits, and even the most independent people suffer when they don't have regular social encounters. No man is an island, as the saying goes. Unfortunately, a lot of people are feeling isolated these days. A 2020 survey found that around 47% of US adults were chronically lonely, and of course the public health measures implemented at the start of the COVID-19 pandemic made many people even more isolated than before.

People who are socially isolated often have physical as well as psychological symptoms. A 1988 study from the University of Michigan found that living without social relationships "constitute[s] a major risk factor for health—rivaling the effects of well-established health risk factors such as cigarette smoking, blood pressure, blood lipids, obesity and physical inactivity."

Social welfare expert Katherine Compitus says that people need social connections in order to thrive, and for some people who lack a human "pack," interacting with a dog can fulfill that need to some extent. "From a simply biological perspective, we literally feel better when we interact with people or animals. We get flooded with a feel-good hormone. When we interact with animals our oxytocin levels rise, and oxytocin is the love hormone. It bonds mothers to children; it's what happens when people fall in love. And when people break up, that's why it hurts so much—they're actually going through oxytocin withdrawal."

Just like dogs can accept both a human pack and a canine pack, people can create a pack that goes beyond their natural family. Certainly, family is normally our first and strongest pack. We bond immediately with our parents and often have close relationships with our siblings and even cousins, grandparents, and other relatives. But in some cases, those family relationships become unhealthy, or people become separated from their family members through relocation, disagreements, or death. When that happens, forming another pack that includes friends and perhaps a life partner can fill the gap—those without a pack can assemble their own. Compitus says, "Family doesn't have to be blood ties. Our community, wherever we find it, whatever we make of it, can be our family."

> In 2005, I packed up my life and moved from Canada to New Zealand, where I had no family and no friends. It was tough. My parents learned to use a computer for the first time so we could have regular video chats, and I used email and social media to stay in touch with my friends back home. But in reality, I needed to build a new pack from scratch. A lack of social contacts is one of the main reasons why immigration fails in many cases. I knew that if I didn't connect with people in New Zealand, I'd end up back in Canada within a year.

> I started by joining an online dating website, where I would eventually meet my future husband (who was also an immigrant to New Zealand). I also joined a local tramping club (tramping is what Kiwis call hiking) to meet people who were interested in the same activities as me. I lived with three housemates so I wouldn't be sitting around alone every night. And once I found work, I met people there too. My new pack didn't replace my lifelong friends and family back home, but they made my life in New Zealand much happier.

How to be happier by finding your pack

Finding a pack—the right pack—can make you happier by giving you the meaningful interactions you need to be mentally healthy and experience positive feelings. One study discovered that good social connections make people happier than money, success, or possessions. And when you put the effort into your pack relationships to make sure they're strong and mutually satisfying, you boost your happiness even more. People have an advantage over dogs in that we have more options for choosing the pack that works best for us.

Dogs don't necessarily get along with every other dog or person they meet, but they bond with the pack members they love the most. It's all about a good fit. You should seek out people for your pack who make you feel better about yourself and fill you with positive emotions. If a pack member makes you feel bad every time you see them, ask yourself whether they should still be in your pack.

Increase your social interactions

It's practically impossible to stay happy without a pack of some kind. But if you don't have an ideal pack already, don't panic. You can still improve your happiness in the meantime by interacting with people you aren't quite as close to. For example, you might get along with some of your colleagues at work well enough to have lunch together, even if you wouldn't share your personal problems with them or invite them to your home. Activities you enjoy can also be a good way to increase your social interactions. If you have a dog, you've probably noticed that other people in your neighborhood with dogs will say hello when you're out for a walk. Why not stop to chat (about your dogs, naturally) for a few minutes?

Compitus suggests that these interactions can help boost your mood in a similar way to having a pack. "You go to a dog park, for example, and you see the same people every day. That's a whole subculture and that's a whole community. And I know plenty of people in dog parks that end up spending a significant amount of time with each other, because their dogs play together. These little daily interactions help us to be connected to other people, to society at large, to our community. It helps us not feel so alone, and so alone in our problems, when we connect with other people."

Ideally, you will be able to find or build a close pack over time and experience the comfort and happiness that come from social intimacy. But in the meantime, less intimate connections are far better than none at all.

Identify your pack

You may not be entirely sure whether you currently have a pack, or whether your pack is a healthy one for you. To identify your pack, ask yourself a few questions: Who are the most important people in your life? Who do you spend the most time with? Who do you ask for advice when you have a problem, or tell first when something exciting happens?

You need to know who your pack is, because these are the people you're counting on to be there for you. Anyone you interact with on a regular basis (and it doesn't need to be in person) could be a member of your pack.

Your pack should be people you feel comfortable sharing personal details with and asking for help. Spending time around them should leave you feeling refreshed and happy. If you are not getting this result from your current pack, you may need to think about making some changes.

Build the right pack for you

Start keeping track of your interactions, maybe on a calendar or in a notebook. Who did you connect with today and how did it go? You can put a scoring system in place if that helps you. On a scale of one to five, how deep was your interaction? How positive was it? How happy did it leave you feeling?

If you find there are people you regularly interact with who leave you feeling worse rather than better, maybe you need to purge them from your pack or give them less of your attention. Happiness coach Kim Strobel warns that you take on the characteristics of the people you're around the most. "I think we have to be conscientious of who we choose to be in our pack. They say you're the average of the five people you spend the most time with. I personally want to be around people who are better than me, because they raise the bar for finding the potential within myself. And so you do need a pack, you need social connections, but you have to make sure that those social connections are on the same vibrational level that you are operating from."

If you're spending a lot of time around people who are always negative, you'll feel that way too. Don't let your pack drag you down; find a pack that lifts you up. Having happy friends has been proven to make people happier. One study found that having a friend who lives within one mile of you who becomes happy makes it 25% more likely that you will also become happy. Finding the right pack should be a top happiness priority.

Be a giver

You might think your pack is there to give you support, and that's what will make you happy. But the old saying "it's better to give than to receive" turns out to be true when your goal is happiness.

Positive psychology expert Shawn Achor says, "It turns out that giving feels better, does more for you, and provides greater returns in the long run than getting support does. Doing something for someone else raises our levels of hope, joy, and happiness."

Think about a time when someone came to you for advice or help with something important and you were able to help them. It feels good, doesn't it? Being there for your pack members helps increase your sense of purpose, and that makes you happy.

Even helping strangers—whether you're doing volunteer work for a charity or buying lunch for someone down on their luck—will boost your mood.

Ideally, your pack members will be there to return the favor when you need support. And if there's a dog in your pack, you can probably count on a friendly ear to listen to your problems (although you might not receive much advice), a furry shoulder to cry on, and a cuddle whenever you need one.

Paws and reflect

- Human brains have evolved for social interaction, and we struggle both mentally and physically when we are isolated.
- Family bonds are our first and often strongest connections, but a pack can include whomever you choose. They should be the people you trust and feel comfortable confiding in.
- You should feel better after spending time with your pack members. If you don't, it may mean you need to remove some people from your pack or spend less time with them.
- You tend to reflect the people around you, so choose to spend time around people you want to be like and who make you feel good about yourself.
- Offering support to members of your pack often feels even better than receiving support from them. Emotional support should go both ways.

Photo credit: Meesiri for Shutterstock

6
Trust the "sniff test"

Pawsitive dogma

You can know things without understanding why you know them. You are aware of just a fraction of the information you take in.

Note from Nuka

If you want to hang with me, you need to pass my sniff test first! If I meet a new dog or human and get a bad feeling about them, I don't sit back and ask why I'm uncomfortable or give them the benefit of the doubt. I bark or back away or whatever I need to do to stay safe! On the other hand, if I like someone, I'm right in there saying hello, nose first and tail wagging. What makes me decide one way or the other? I dunno—it's automatic.

People seem to have the same instant reaction when they meet somebody for the first time, but I don't think you trust your own feelings. You put up with people who make you uncomfortable, even though I can see you kind of backing away. The weird thing is, you keep on putting up with those people long after you should know better. Apparently you're afraid of upsetting the bad person. It's weird! If you trusted your sniff test like dogs do, you could avoid a lot of bad experiences.

What the dog experts say

Dogs trust their noses above all else. That's why they are so keen to sniff a new dog before they decide whether to play together. That first sniff can tell them about another dog's health, sexual state, and even their state of mind. But sometimes they don't even get to that stage because there are visual cues that can be read from a distance. A dog with body language that's either aggressive or very fearful is off-putting to other dogs. Dogs that weren't well socialized as puppies sometimes give off the wrong signals, and other dogs will react badly to their awkwardness. All of this plays out in the blink of an eye.

Dogs have also learned to read humans almost instantly. Again, this is partly noticing our body language and facial expressions and partly noticing how we smell. Is the person stiff or relaxed? Leaning forward to dominate or squatting down to interact? Staring intently or glancing softly? Do they smell aggressive or calm?

6. TRUST THE "SNIFF TEST"

You've probably heard that dogs can "smell fear." This is literally true. We give off pheromones (even though we're not well equipped to smell them) that indicate our state of mind, just like dogs do. And it turns out that the smells of a human who's afraid and a human who's angry are very similar. When a dog reacts aggressively to someone who is afraid of dogs, it could be that the dog thinks the person is angry and therefore a threat. Dog behavior expert Alexandra Horowitz says, "We spontaneously sweat under stress, and our perspiration carries a note of our odor on it: that's the first clue to the dog. Adrenaline, used by the body to gear up for a good sprint away from something dangerous, is unscented to us, but not to the sensitive sniffer of the dog."

In fact, we've become so convinced that dogs know who to trust and who not to, many of us will take our cues from them. Social welfare expert Katherine Compitus sometimes has a dog in the room when she meets with clients who have trouble trusting people. For therapy to be effective, the client must trust the therapist. Compitus has found that dogs can help build that trust faster. "If there's a dog in the room, even from their first time walking in, the clients see this dog is happy, this dog is well fed, this dog is cared for. So they infer this person, this therapist, is going to care for *me* as well. It speeds up that building of trust, that connection between the therapist and the client."

Dogs are also very well attuned to the reactions of their human companions. You may not even be aware that you're reacting noticeably to a new person or a dog, but your dog is watching you and taking note. Horowitz says, "They may seem to recognize someone who is not to be trusted. What this ability might come down to is their close looking at our looking. If you feel hesitant about an approaching stranger, you reveal it, however unintentionally."

Dog behavior expert Ian Dunbar agrees that our dogs are carefully watching us for cues. "Most dogs can read their owner's innermost thoughts as easily as an open book published in large type. The dog perceives and assesses literally thousands of subtle social cues from our tone of voice, facial expressions, body language, movement, body temperature, body odor and galvanic skin response (sweating), and then it computes most likely outcomes at lightning speed."

Between their own perceptions and their reading of our reactions, dogs make a very quick judgment about how to react to a new person or dog. It feels instantaneous to us—but to our dogs, identifying a potential threat is something you shouldn't wait on. By the time you've thought it through, you could be under attack.

> Marlowe reacts to different people in different ways, and if he doesn't like them he lets them know. For example, when I was getting quotes to have my kitchen renovated, I had a designer come over to take a look. As soon as he stepped into the house, Marlowe started barking at him. Marlowe didn't calm down even after it was clear that this man was allowed to be there and he took a seat at our table. My husband had to take Marlowe to another part of the house so I could meet with the designer.

> What was Marlowe reacting to? If I had to guess, it was probably body language. This guy was a self-centered know-it-all. His posture and gait probably looked aggressive or dominant. Our conversation about my kitchen reno involved him talking for 20 minutes straight before he asked me a single question about what I wanted. When I got his proposed design, it included a feature I specifically told him I didn't want. Needless to say, I didn't end up hiring him. I could have saved myself some time and frustration by listening to Marlowe in the first place.

What the happiness experts say

You may have heard a lot of mixed messages about how to deal with your visceral reactions to people. Some people say to trust your instincts (or your "gut reaction"), while others say not to judge a book by its cover and to give people the benefit of the doubt. How accurate are your subconscious reactions to people? Should you rely on them without question?

Social psychologist Jonathan Haidt says that, just like dogs, "we humans have a like-o-meter too, and it's always running. Its influence is subtle, but careful experiments show that you have a like-dislike reaction to everything you are experiencing, even if you're not aware of the experience."

Emma Seppälä, a happiness and emotional intelligence expert, says that when people have a "gut reaction," it's a physical response to how they think the other person is feeling. For example, if you sense that someone is angry (even if they're trying to hide it), you will feel a bit riled up yourself without being able to put your finger on the reason. She says, "We all have a built-in empathy system that is extremely sensitive; it is faster and more automatic than our ability to reason—much like a reflex. Even when we don't consciously know it, someone else's emotion or pain registers physiologically within us."

Your reactions to people result from what you observe about them, whether you're aware of those observations or not. The more you can perceive in an instant about someone, the more accurate your sniff test is likely to be. Horowitz was fascinated by the idea that two people could observe the same things in completely different ways, and explored this idea in her book, *On Looking*. She discovered that her seemingly instinctive reactions to people could sometimes be explained by another person's more expert perception. During a walk she took with a physician, people who simply appeared a bit "off" somehow to Horowitz were instantly diagnosed by the physician with a likely condition that affected their gait, posture, or other physical characteristics. Although her reaction seemed like intuition, there was a physical explanation for it.

Since it's based on real observations, the sniff test seems like something you could get better at with practice—and that appears to be true. You can become a better sniffer! Look at people who use it in their jobs every day—for example, people who work at border crossings or airports. They learn how to spot people acting "suspicious" and select them for questioning. They are trained to do this by looking for things like sweating, avoiding eye contact, evasive answers to questions, and so on. If you pay more attention to these kinds of signals, you might also form more accurate opinions about people faster.

People are always communicating their intentions and their feelings and you constantly receive those communications, but most people tend to dismiss them. According to Compitus, "Society teaches us to suppress our natural instincts. Most communication is nonverbal—I think it's 80% or 90% nonverbal—but we've been conditioned and taught to not pay attention to that, 'for the greater good.' Give people the benefit of the doubt, you know? And I think that, just as dogs trust their instincts, we really need to trust our instincts more."

Identifying the people who make us uncomfortable is only the first step, though. We also need to give ourselves permission to act on that and to decide not to spend time with those people or allow them into our lives. Happiness coach Kim Strobel says, "One of the things we need to try to nurture within ourselves is being conscientious and listening to the whispers. I think we are allowed to make conscious choices, even if they disappoint someone else. Dogs inherently do that, and we actually have that same internal guidance system inside of us, but we shove it away. I think we have to quit personalizing it. Why do we think that we should like *everybody*?"

It should seem obvious that you won't like everybody you meet. Some of the people you don't like might be perfectly nice people; they just don't "click" with you. Giving yourself permission to choose who you want to be around, and to trust your feelings toward a person—even if you can't logically explain them—will eliminate some of the things that stand in the way of being happy.

> Have you ever tried speed dating? When I was single, this was a trendy way to meet people. You'd go to a bar or restaurant with a bunch of tables for two set up, and one set of people (either the women or the men, for straight events) would stay seated in the same spot, while the other set would rotate to the next table every two or three minutes. Can you decide in two or three minutes whether you want to date someone? I was amazed by how quickly I formed an opinion during my mini-dates. In fact, there were times when those few minutes seemed to drag on because we'd both clearly decided in the first few seconds that there was no connection between us. It was an interesting exercise in developing my sniff-test skills. Admittedly, my accuracy may not have been the best—I never did launch a new relationship at these events.

How to be happier by trusting the "sniff test"

How is mastering the sniff test going to make you happier? By giving you a short cut to choosing the right people to surround yourself with. As we discussed in "Find your pack," your happiness is closely tied to those you spend the most time with. If you feel uncomfortable around people, you could be draining your emotional reserves and robbing yourself of happiness without realizing it. Your pack should make you feel better, not worse. When your sniff test is working well, you'll feel more confident about deciding who's in and who's out.

Get in touch with your instincts

Some people are naturally attuned to their inner reactions. They often refer to themselves as "instinctive" or "intuitive." Because they have had mostly good results from trusting their initial feelings, they don't bother waiting for external confirmation before they act. This has its roots in our evolution, back when we were not at the top of the food chain. Humans had to be constantly alert to potential dangers, like predators stalking us. If we stopped to think about it for too long, we'd be someone's lunch. So we developed an instinctive response to subtle clues that something was not quite right.

You may not be one of those highly intuitive people, but you can learn to listen to your own intuition by practicing. Awareness is the first step. When you are introduced to someone new, take a moment at the end of the encounter to notice how you feel. Are you stressed? Happy? Do you want to see that person again or would you try to avoid running into them?

Once you establish how they made you feel, see if you can pinpoint anything about them that might be the underlying cause. Did they seem interested in you or distracted? Did they seem honest or evasive? Did they look relaxed and comfortable, or did they seem nervous or aggressive? Did they smile or make eye contact? Did their smile seem genuine?

If you find this difficult, try it first with someone who already makes you uncomfortable. Maybe someone at work you find unpleasant, or a friend of a friend you always hope won't be joining you. See if you can pin down what bothers you about that person. Do they interrupt when you're speaking? Put other people down? Look away while you're talking to them?

You might instantly dislike some people simply because they remind you of someone else who had a negative effect on your life. Our memories have deep, lasting emotional effects on us, and they can trigger a powerful subconscious response when something reminds us of our past suffering. Perhaps your friend's friend has the same smile as your ex-partner; without realizing why, you just can't stand that person. Maybe they use the same cologne and the smell triggers you emotionally. Instinctive reactions can sometimes be unfair to the other person, but that doesn't change the fact that you're feeling unhappy around them. It's possible the person will win you over and you'll be able to override that initial reaction, but it may not ever happen.

Try to identify the things that affect your instinctive reactions to people so you can be more aware of them and use them intentionally, instead of just hoping your instincts are accurate. The more you understand what's making people pass or fail your sniff test, the more you can use it to increase your happiness by including the right people in your life.

Most of this chapter has focused on using the sniff test as an early warning against people who make you uncomfortable, but it can also be a positive test. Have you ever met someone at work, at school, or at a social event, and right from that first meeting they felt like an old friend? That person passed your sniff test with flying colors! Just like the negative test, you may be reacting to body language and facial expressions, or that person could remind you of someone you already like. Whatever the reason, it's often a sign that this person has the capacity to make you happier. You could say that love at first sight is just an extreme version of passing the sniff test.

Give yourself permission to choose

Giving yourself permission to use the sniff test to make decisions can help you make happiness your top priority. Sure, you could make a list of pros and cons about a person to help you decide whether they're good for you, but you might find that trying to reason with yourself that way actually leads you to prioritize other factors over your own happiness—factors like whether that person is close to someone you love, whether they will be difficult to avoid, or whether they have some influence over your life. When you consider how happy you feel around that person as the most important factor, your decisions might look quite different.

As an example, let's say you are interviewed for a really interesting job. Your interviewer is the person you'd be directly working for in this position. You immediately feel uncomfortable and awkward during the interview, and you leave feeling as if they didn't like you. If you're offered the job, should you take it? Think about how it will feel to work closely with this person every day. Will you be excited to head in to work, or will you dread it? Will the interesting job make up for the stress of spending every day with someone who makes you unhappy?

Find your sweet spot

Everyone has a different level of trust in their sniff test, and different experiences with how accurate it is. Those people who call themselves "intuitive" are happy to rely on the sniff test most of the time. They can give you plenty of examples of times when trusting their intuition brought them a great reward or allowed them to avoid a disaster. But of course, we all suffer from "confirmation bias": we notice the things that confirm what we already believe to be true and ignore things that contradict those beliefs. People who always trust their intuition may conveniently forget the times when it led them down the wrong path.

Other people have very little trust in their sniff test. They need to be absolutely sure of the facts before they make a decision. Although this is admirable in many ways, they might suffer through a lot of unpleasant situations for longer than necessary while they collect evidence.

The smoothest road to happiness likely lies somewhere in between. When your sniff test kicks in immediately and sends a strong message, there's probably something to it. If you can teach yourself to be more observant and take in those early clues about new people and situations, you can make better decisions more quickly. Just remember to make your happiness the main goal of those decisions.

Paws and reflect

- You have a built-in "like-o-meter" that helps you form an instant opinion of a new person.
- Some people trust what they call their "intuition," which is their sniff test. Others resist it because they think people deserve the benefit of the doubt. But ignoring your sniff test for too long can erode your happiness.
- Paying attention to subtle signals like body language, facial expressions, and eye contact can help your sniff test become more accurate.
- The sniff test can be either positive or negative. You can use it to identify people you'll hit it off with immediately as well as people you'd rather avoid.
- Giving yourself permission to use your instinctive reaction to someone as a deciding factor can help you make decisions that prioritize your happiness.

Photo credit: Ulrike Mai for Pixabay

7
Bark, don't bite

Pawsitive dogma

When you bury your anger deep inside, you compress it like a spring until it explodes with extraordinary force.

Message from Marlowe

My humans sometimes get embarrassed or upset when I growl or bark, but asking me not to do it is like asking a person not to talk. How else can I tell you all the important stuff you need to know? Our home could be in danger (I see you coming, delivery guy!) or something could be scaring me. When I bark, I'm letting you know what's on my mind so you won't be surprised by what I do next. I'd much rather bark when something's wrong than sit there *letting it get worse and worse until I need to bite to protect myself.*

I think people don't like to bark because it feels rude. Instead you just sit there quietly, even when something's bothering you. Why not bark right away? Why wait until it's so bad that it becomes a really big deal and you're super angry? Maybe if you even just growled a little, the other humans would get the hint.

What the dog experts say

Dogs are sometimes accused of biting a person or another dog "out of the blue," but often they sent clear warnings that were ignored. Dogs don't want to fight—who does? It's dangerous and it usually doesn't accomplish much. Instead, they'd rather sort it out before it turns into a real fight. To do this, dogs have developed a multistage system of communication to resolve situations they're unhappy about.

Dog behavior expert Stanley Coren says there are distinct stages when one dog is telling another dog to back off. The first stage is a snarl or growl, and the next is a bark. If the offending dog doesn't take the hint, the first dog might snap their jaws at the other dog, without making any contact. If the dog still feels threatened, they'll progress to a controlled bite that makes contact with the other dog but doesn't break the skin. If none of that ends the disagreement, a real bite is the next stage.

7. BARK, DON'T BITE   93

Dogs also have distinctive barks for communicating important information to humans or other dogs. Researchers have tried to interpret some of these barks by analyzing thousands of them, recorded during specific activities. The scenarios they studied were when a stranger rang the doorbell, when the dogs were locked outside, or while they played. They found the stranger barks were the lowest in pitch and the harshest, which means they would travel long distances to alert others to the danger. Loneliness barks had a higher frequency and came one at a time with long breaks between them, perhaps waiting for a response from other dogs. Play barks were also high frequency but happened closer together, to express the dogs' excitement to nearby playmates.

A good rule of thumb is that the lower the pitch of a growl or bark, the more threatening the dog is trying to sound. If a low growl turns into a low bark, you should be very concerned that if you approach that dog they might bite.

Although some people punish their dogs for barking, and some even have surgery performed on their dogs to make it impossible for them to bark, this is a bad idea. A dog who can't bark can't warn you when they're feeling threatened. Instead of biting being their last line of defense, it becomes their *only* line of defense. That's when a dog bite truly comes "out of the blue," but it should never have to be that way.

Nuka barks at the front window whenever dogs or people are walking past. She sounds the alarm from the moment she sees (or hears) a potential intruder until they disappear around a corner. I work at home, so this can get pretty annoying. I can't blame her; she's just trying to keep us all safe. But I've realized that ignoring her isn't the best solution, because she assumes I'm not aware of the threat and keeps going. (And yelling at her doesn't work either. Then we're *both* barking.) Instead, I'll pause what I'm doing and go to the front window. Then I'll thank her for alerting me and make a show of looking outside to assess the threat myself and assure her it's all safe. Once she sees that her human is on the case, she can relax and go back to her pillow knowing that her job is done.

What the happiness experts say

Just like dogs, most people prefer to avoid a nasty confrontation if they can. Unfortunately, some problems won't just go away if you ignore them. You have to react. And the earlier you do, the less drastic your reaction probably needs to be—you can growl rather than bite. But instead, many people suppress their feelings of discomfort, irritation, and anger.

It can be difficult to put your emotional needs first and stand up for yourself when it will make someone else uncomfortable. You might be allowing people to do things to you that you would never allow them to do to your friends or family. Social welfare expert Katherine Compitus says that self-care is disappearing in our society because we're told the needs of others should come before our own. "We need to take care of ourselves *before* we can take care of anyone else. And somehow this is a message we've lost along the way. We think it's more polite to put other people first and suppress our needs, and then we feel badly about it." Instead, she says, you need to be your own best friend. "Why would anybody else respect you if you're not respecting yourself?"

It might sound counterintuitive, but to be happier you might need to express your anger more often. Research has shown that "suppressing negative emotions on a regular basis actually makes people experience more negative emotions and less positive emotions." According to happiness and emotional intelligence expert Emma Seppälä, people who suppress their negative feelings have lower self-esteem, are more pessimistic and more likely to have depression, and even their memory may be affected. Basically, holding in your bad feelings is bad for you.

Happiness coach Kim Strobel thinks we've been conditioned to feel bad about admitting we're unhappy. "I think many times, in close relationships, we think it's supposed to be all wonderful all the time. But what do we see dogs do? Dogs get into it with each other. Even if they're the closest of pals, they'll take it too far and they'll squabble. But for humans, if we squabble, it's a friendship divorce!"

There's no reason you can't learn from dogs and approach your disagreements in escalating stages, so you can try to settle things with as little conflict as possible while still getting the result you want.

Bridget Grenville-Cleave, a positive psychology expert, describes how anger can build up when you don't let it out. "Sometimes anger starts as a low-lying, slow-burning sense of frustration which, if not dealt with effectively, can build up over time like the steam in a pressure cooker, then suddenly explode, leading to actions which may be harmful to oneself as well as others." Instead, she suggests, you should recognize those early stages of frustration and take action right away so you can return to a more positive mental state.

When I lived with my first long-term boyfriend, he worked in the restaurant industry. That meant late hours a lot of the time, which put a strain on our relationship. One summer, he seemed to be spending more and more time with his co-workers and I felt like we barely saw one another. Not only was he working late, but at the end of his shift he would go out with the crew until the wee hours.

One night, he called me as his shift was ending and asked if it was OK if he went out with his work friends somewhere. I said sure and hung up the phone. Then I burst into tears. I had been feeling terrible about how things were going, but I was avoiding a tough conversation about our relationship. I pulled out a sheet of paper and began writing a note that began, "It's not OK …" and I told him what was no longer working for me. This "bark" gave us a chance to talk things out, rather than waiting for the whole relationship to fall apart.

How to be happier by barking, not biting

Lashing out at people (the human equivalent of biting "out of the blue") can have serious consequences. It could cost you your job, relationship, or friendship, or potentially even land you in jail. None of that is going to make you very happy. Here are some ways to take care of your conflicts before they reach the boiling point.

Speak up

In an effort to make yourself happier, you might be trying to ignore things that aren't going well. You may think this will help you avoid getting angry or upset (and having negative thoughts), but as the research shows, it will actually make you even more upset. Pretending to be happy isn't the same as being happy.

When something upsets you, think about how to stand up for yourself. Happiness expert Stephanie Staples suggests that you ask yourself, "'What does being assertive look like in this situation?' Maybe you don't have to just passively sit back and take it, and maybe you don't have to jump down their throat and be rude and mean, but what does being assertive look like?"

So, what *does* being assertive look like? It depends on the situation you're facing. For example, if your boss is giving you more and more work, and you are already too busy, being assertive can mean asking for a meeting with them to decide which tasks are the highest priority and which ones can wait. If you are a parent, being assertive might mean limiting the number of after-school activities for your kids, so you don't spend every evening driving them around. Maybe being assertive means telling a friend or acquaintance that you disagree with their opinion on something, and expressing your own opinion. Maybe it's telling them you found their comment upsetting and explaining why. And sometimes being assertive means asking for an apology.

Pinpoint the problem

Conflicts can get out of hand when the people involved don't stick to the subject they're disagreeing about. Instead, it becomes about the other person being horrible and thoughtless, or the fact that they *always* do this or *never* think about that. Soon, you're arguing about anything and everything instead of trying to settle your current disagreement.

The first step is to ask yourself what is really making you angry. Often, the incident that triggers an angry reaction is not the real cause of your anger—it's just the final straw. When irritants have gone unchecked for a long time, it can feel like *everything* is wrong. Before you go into full-on fight mode, try to assess what the real problem is. Are you actually mad that your partner waited too long to book your vacation and your favorite hotel is full? Or are you simply stressed out because it's been way too long since you had a break and you really need to get away and relax?

Try to put borders around the issue you need to settle at the beginning of any disagreement. If you're upset about your kids leaving dirty laundry on the floor, have a discussion about leaving laundry on the floor, not a rant about an entire generation of lazy, good-for-nothing, entitled kids who spend too much time playing video games.

Some problems really are "big picture" issues. But arguing about those is unlikely to be productive when you're ready to explode with anger. Wait until you're calm to address large-scale problems. Maybe a family meeting is needed. Or perhaps you need a neutral party to facilitate the discussion, like a therapist or a counselor.

Once you identify a specific problem and focus directly on that, the conversation can be much more civilized. You may still need to growl to make it clear that you're unhappy with the situation, but you might be able to avoid barking, or at least work things out before anyone gets bitten.

Focus on solutions

Dogs have pretty simple solutions to most of their disagreements. Get off my property. Don't take that bone. Stop staring at me like that. Human problems aren't always that easy to fix, but by keeping your discussion focused on the issue at hand, you can then look at possible solutions that will let you get back to being happy.

Once you've expressed why you're upset or disappointed, try to shift the focus to the outcome you'd like to see. Harping on about being upset doesn't move you any closer to the end of the conflict. Suggesting a solution is much more productive.

Sometimes you're faced with someone who believes they are completely right—someone who doesn't want to find a solution because they think nothing is wrong with the way things are. If you can't sway the other person, you may need to take action on your own. Think about what is within your control. How can you change the situation for the better, from your point of view? Trying to change another person is often an impossible task, but maybe you can change how you interact with that person to reduce their negative effect on you.

In short, fix what you can by having a rational discussion about it. (And rational discussions don't need to avoid the topic of your feelings, if the problem is making you feel upset, frustrated, or angry.) What you can't fix together, you may need to try to fix on your own. Either way, dealing with the problem before it becomes overwhelming will help you prevent a huge conflict and the wave of negative emotions that will otherwise take over your brain. Find your way back to happiness as early in the situation as you can.

Paws and reflect

- 🐾 The sooner you react to a situation that's bothering you, the less drastic your reaction likely needs to be. You can growl, rather than bark or bite.

- 🐾 Standing up for yourself is a form of self-care and self-respect. Making other people happy at your own expense will eventually make you less capable of caring for them.

- 🐾 You can disagree with someone or ask them to change something without destroying your relationship with them. But this is more likely to work if you speak up before your frustration and anger become overwhelming.

- 🐾 Try to deal with one issue at a time, rather than lumping everything together. It's easier to solve a specific problem than to change a whole relationship.

- 🐾 For "big picture" issues, you may need to seek help from a neutral third party, like a counselor or therapist.

- 🐾 Once you've expressed what you're unhappy about, try to shift the discussion to possible solutions rather than staying focused on the problem.

Photo credit: Pixabay

8
Shake it off

Pawsitive dogma

Don't let your negative thoughts weigh you down. Shake them off and free yourself to find happiness again.

Note from Nuka

I admit it. Sometimes I don't get along with absolutely all the other dogs I meet. Now and then another dog crosses the line and we have a few angry growls and maybe snap at each other. My humans get upset and usually want to drag me away from the other dog. But the growling and snapping only last for a few seconds. As soon as it ends, I just do a big shake and get rid of all that tension so I can relax and have some more fun. A little bit of stress doesn't have to ruin my whole day!

I don't get why humans hold on to their stress and anger and negative stuff for so long. Wouldn't you rather be happy? Just shake it out of your system and let it go like dogs do. Staying angry or stressed out won't help anything. The sooner you move on, the sooner you'll be happy again.

What the dog experts say

If you've spent a lot of time around dogs, you've seen the body shake. It looks like they're shaking water off themselves, but they're not wet. The whole body gets involved, from head to tail. There are a lot of events that end with a body shake: scrapping with another dog, chasing after an animal, or even just intently smelling something on the ground. Whenever they do it, dogs are basically resetting their mood back to neutral and getting ready to move on to something new—they are saying, "Well, that's over. What's next?"

This is an important social skill for dogs because it helps them avoid serious fights. Dog behavior expert Ian Dunbar says being able to shake off tense moments and get back to a positive state is something puppies learn early. "How to recover quickly, or bounce back, from a disagreement and resume playing is one of the most important skills pups have to learn before they can confidently enjoy the world of big dogs." Puppies who fail to learn this quickly enough will be taught an unpleasant lesson when an adult dog tells them off. But just as disappointing, when the puppy can't shake off a negative encounter, they miss out on the chance to play more. And playing, of course, is one of a puppy's favorite things to do.

Shaking works because it forces the dog's muscles to relax and release. According to dog behavior expert Stanley Coren, "When we look at anxiety or fear, one of the things we talk about is being 'tense.' And that's literally what happens—your muscles tense. It turns out that you can't feel tense if your muscles are relaxed. And that's all the dogs are doing, just unlocking their muscles." By shaking the tension out of their bodies, dogs are leaving their anxious feelings behind so they can feel happy and relaxed again.

> We arrived at the park one day, and some neighbors were there playing fetch with their goldendoodle. We let Nuka off leash to play with the doodle because they generally got along well. But the doodle was not happy to share her ball. When Nuka looked like she was going to grab it, the other dog growled and snapped. Nuka took offense and snapped back, and it looked like a fight was going to break out. But instead, the doodle took her ball and trotted back to her designated thrower. Nuka did a big body shake and decided this game wasn't fun anymore, so we walked on. Dog friendships don't have to end because of one disagreement. After a good shake, everyone can forget about it and go back to being happy.

What the happiness experts say

Humans are decidedly non-dog-like when it comes to letting go of negative thoughts. We cling to them long after the incident that caused them is over—sometimes for years. We often wish for revenge or obsess over how we were wronged. Unfortunately, it's part of being human. Psychology researcher Christopher Boehm found that "compared to other animals, humans are particularly prone to retaliation. Reactivity feeds conflict, which feeds reactivity, in an escalating cycle of grievance, grudge, and payback." Shaking off the bad stuff is not in our nature; we need to work at it.

The problem is, the more we try to stop thinking about something that's been bothering us, the more we can't help thinking about it. Maybe you've experienced this. As a simple example, let's say there's a spider high up on the wall behind you and you hate spiders. You tell yourself not to think about the spider because it's not close enough to do anything to you. But you soon find that, instead, you are quickly becoming obsessed with the spider you're trying not to look at.

Researchers set up studies where participants were asked to try very hard *not* to think about a particular thing. The more people tried to suppress that thought, the more it came flooding back into their minds. Social psychologist Jonathan Haidt says, "Whenever one pursues a goal, a part of the mind automatically monitors progress, so that it can order corrections or know when success has been achieved. But when the goal is mental, it backfires." Since your brain is trying to monitor whether you are successfully *not* thinking about the thing, you end up thinking about it again and again.

What happens when you tell people the story of a bad experience to get sympathy from them or to ponder how you could have handled things better? Happiness expert Stephanie Staples says people often think they'll feel better if they tell their friends about something that made them angry or sad. But they end up repeating the story over and over and reliving the whole thing, which can make them feel almost as angry and upset as they were when it first happened. Some people don't realize that when they tell that story, they don't feel better—they feel worse. "So maybe it's time to stop telling that story," she suggests. In other words, shake it off and move on to something new. Stop intentionally reliving your bad experiences.

Social welfare expert Katherine Compitus believes you sometimes need to forgive yourself or stop blaming yourself for what happened before you can shake it off. "If we just learn to accept things as is, then we can move forward. When we stop judging ourselves and our world, it removes that burden of responsibility on us, that we have to fix everything. We can't fix the past. We simply cannot."

Replaying your negative thoughts is certainly not going to lead to more feelings of happiness. Instead, you can learn resilience, which is the act of bouncing back to a positive state after a negative experience. Whether you think of it as "shaking" or "bouncing," it's the act of leaving those past tensions behind and not letting them ruin the present for you.

Like other animals, you have a "fight or flight" response that makes you more alert and tense when you feel threatened. It makes you ready to face your immediate problems, but in order to move on you need to exit that "emergency" state.

Happiness and emotional intelligence expert Emma Seppälä uses the example of how an antelope demonstrates resilience. When antelopes are chased by a predator, their fight or flight response allows them to identify the danger and flee quickly, and hopefully survive. But if antelopes stayed in that state of high alert all the time, they would be exhausted and their bodies wouldn't work as well. They wouldn't digest their food properly or recover enough of their strength to face the next threat. They are resilient because they switch back to "rest and digest" mode once the danger is gone. They don't spend the rest of their day replaying the danger in their minds.

Admittedly, shaking it off is a hard one for me. I tend to hold on to bad experiences (especially ones that involve rejection) for far too long, and they can damage my self-esteem. For instance, my first book, *Sex in a Tent: A Wild Couple's Guide to Getting Naughty in Nature*, was all about relationships and had quite a lot of sexual content. After its release, I would occasionally search online to see if the book was getting any publicity or reviews I wasn't aware of. One day I stumbled across a comment on a review of the book. The commenter had done an image search using my name (ick!) and decided he would never take sex advice from someone who looked like me (no need to repeat his exact words here). I'm no supermodel, but having a stranger specifically call out my appearance really hurt. It took a lot of effort not to respond to the comment. (Dude, have you ever heard of world-famous sex expert Dr. Ruth Westheimer? She's in her 90s and people still want her advice!) I'm sure he never expected me to see his comment. The best thing to do was just shake it off. Plenty of other people had lovely things to say about the book, including the reviewer. But the fact that I still recall the comment means I never completely succeeded in dismissing it from my mind.

How to be happier by shaking it off

If humans are naturally inclined to hold on to anger, fear, anxiety, and other negative emotions, how can you learn to be more dog-like and shake them off? People spend so much time feeling tense and anxious that it's easy to reach a point where you aren't even aware of it anymore. It's just part of who you are. Awareness is the first step to turning off those negative emotions and giving yourself a chance to feel happy. Like anything else, it's going to take practice and you'll have to replace some old habits with new tricks. Let's look at some steps you can take to start working on this right away.

Don't just replay the past, learn from it

When you find yourself replaying a negative event, such as an argument you had with someone earlier (maybe an hour ago, maybe a decade ago), stop and take a moment to recognize what you're doing. Ask yourself what prompted you to think of it just now. You can do the same thing for any memory that makes you angry or tense. Why are you thinking about the disappointment of when you were turned down for a raise, when your ideas were rejected in a meeting, or when someone important to you let you down? Is there something currently happening to you that reminded you of that past event?

If the past experience is relevant to something happening now, try to shift your focus to the lessons you learned or what you could do differently this time. Try to picture a more positive scenario playing out. When you go into a situation expecting a negative outcome because that's what happened last time, it becomes a self-fulfilling prophecy. You might even subconsciously sabotage yourself. Instead, think about how well it could potentially go and try to make that happen.

If it doesn't help you, get rid of it

As I mentioned, telling yourself to stop thinking about something doesn't work. But if your past conflicts or traumas are keeping your mind occupied with negative thoughts, you need to find a way to put them aside. Often, there is no good reason to keep thinking of something stressful again and again, but it can be very hard to stop.

There are several methods you can try that might help you release your mind from its negative obsessions and give it a chance to let in more positive thoughts. The first one seems ridiculously simple, but it is effective nonetheless: breathe.

Breathing exercises can help you release tension in your body and even rebalance your hormone levels so you aren't drowning in stress hormones. You can use meditation or yoga to do this, or simply focus on your breathing and take slow, deep breaths several times whenever you notice you're tense or anxious.

You can also try out a dog's approach to the problem and physically shake it off. A lot of people find exercise helpful when their mind is stuck on something stressful. You can try running, weight training, dancing, boxing (particularly satisfying when you're angry at someone), or your favorite cardio class.

You can also try stretching, which will actively release your tense muscles. By making your body relax, you send the signal to your brain to relax too. If you're stretching out your body, you can't be in "fight or flight" mode, and that message travels through your nervous system and tells your brain that all is well and you are safe. If you need help, get a relaxing massage or ask your partner to rub your shoulders or your feet.

Another remedy that has become popular is "forest bathing," which simply means going somewhere you can be surrounded by nature. If you don't have a forest nearby, you can go to any park where you'll be exposed to trees and grass. Listen to the wind blowing through the leaves. Smell the trees, flowers, and grass. Focus on nature's shapes, textures, sounds, and smells. And don't forget your deep breathing, which will help you take in the oxygen the plants are producing. This option takes some discipline on your part, because it's quite easy to find yourself walking through the forest thinking about your problems. If you do that, keep catching yourself and bringing your mind back to the present.

If you're struggling to turn off your negative thoughts, use a distraction to pull yourself out of your own head. Putting on some music that makes you feel good is one approach, or even singing a happy song yourself (the shower is an acceptable venue). Watch a movie or TV show you love and that reminds you of a happy time. Call a friend who always makes you laugh or feel good about yourself. But if you do this, avoid getting into a long conversation about *why* you need to be cheered up—that is the opposite of shaking it off!

If you can get your negative thoughts to stop playing on an endless loop, your mind will be ready to take in more positive and useful thoughts that can make you happy. You'll be able to start living in the moment, wagging your tail, learning new tricks, and so on because you will no longer be trapped in a cycle of negativity.

If you've been working on this and your negative mindset is stubbornly sticking around because it's rooted in traumatic experiences or serious underlying issues, you may need support from a professional, like a therapist or counselor. We'll talk about that later on, in "Dig below the surface."

Paws and reflect

- 🐾 People tend to dwell more on negative experiences and thoughts because of the brain's negativity bias, which makes it difficult to shake things off and move on.

- 🐾 Telling people about your negative experience can make you feel bad about it all over again, rather than getting it "off your chest."

- 🐾 Becoming more resilient can help you recover faster from bad experiences and get back to feeling happy.

- 🐾 Instead of just replaying the bad experience, try to identify what you've learned from it and imagine how it could go better next time.

- 🐾 Use physical movement to shake yourself out of your funk: breathe deeply, stretch, exercise, or get out into nature.

- 🐾 You can shake off a bad experience by distracting yourself: listen to music, call a friend who cheers you up, watch a favorite movie, or read a book.

Photo credit: Rita Dixon "Maggie Rose"

9
Go for a walk

Pawsitive dogma

Step into the world. Be a part of it. You cannot live inside your head all the time and be happy.

Message from Marlowe

Going for a walk is the best thing I do all day! Most of the time, I'm just sitting around the house waiting for something to happen or having naps. It gets old pretty fast. It's not just that I need exercise (although apparently I do 'cause I'm a bit chonky). Going for a walk also exercises my brain. On walks there are different things to smell, see, and do. They get me out into the big world. Walks are super important for making me happy!

People need to get out and walk too, but I think you forget sometimes. How can you forget about walks—they're awesome! You just sit there looking at screens all day. But if you want your body and your brain to be at their best, you need to get up and experience the whole world around you. Staying stuck at home or at work makes it way harder to be happy.

What the dog experts say

If you think about it, dogs spend most of their lives just waiting for us. It's not surprising that they get excited (maybe even overexcited) when it's time to go for a walk. This is the highlight of their day, and yet we tend to rush them through it so we can get on with our other tasks. Your dog doesn't care how far they get on their walk, or how many calories they burn. They're just happy to be on the go with their human, enjoying the journey.

Dog behavior expert Alexandra Horowitz advises people to set aside their own goals for the walk and "consider the walk your dog wants." That can mean letting your dog choose your route, letting them sniff things, going back and forth instead of in a straight line, and stopping to greet the people and dogs you encounter along the way.

Walks are the best time for a dog to collect experiences and stimulate their mind. You can even give them new challenges to conquer by doing a bit of "doggie parkour." Get them to jump or climb over fallen logs, walk along low walls, jump on and off the curb as you walk, or anything that helps them interact with the environment in a more complex way.

With enough mental distractions, even a short walk around the block will provide dogs with the stimulation they need. Mental work can be as tiring for a dog as physical effort, so if you don't have time for a long outing, make it an intense mental workout and your dog will still be happy to nap when you get home. In fact, if a dog is physically unable to go for a long walk (because of illness, age, or disability), mentally challenging activities can be essential for keeping them in a positive mood.

Dog behavior expert Stanley Coren says that going for walks around the neighborhood is also important to dogs because it helps them "establish their place" in the larger world. By walking the streets, they get to know the area where they live. They learn about the other dogs who walk the same streets (by either meeting them or smelling their pee on the ground), where the smells wafting through the air are coming from, and how to navigate back home from different places.

Dog trainer Nicole Barnett suggests that for some dogs, the definition of a "walk" might be very different from what we think of. A dog with a lot of fear or anxiety might be happier walking up and down their own block than trying to cover any distance. For older dogs who feel pain when they walk, simply sniffing around the park or lying in a favorite grassy spot might be their best version of a walk. For other dogs, maybe it's splashing in the surf on a local beach, or catching a flying disc in the park.

Dogs who don't go on walks or outings can be socially isolated and mentally understimulated, not to mention physically unhealthy. Walking isn't just about a bathroom break—it's a big part of a dog's well-being.

Nuka is our walk leader. Because her knees have been not-so-great for most of her life—and it's often hard to tell how sore she might be because she's so excited to get out for her walks—we let her decide what kind of walk she feels like. Once she realized that she had this power, she really embraced it. When we leave the house, I'm quite sure she usually has a detailed route in mind. If we fail to follow her planned path, she stops and whines until we go the right way. She'll sometimes guide us straight to a place where she found some food on the ground a day or two before, or to a house where some nice people gave her attention. She'll stop to visit her dog friends at their houses and be quite disappointed if they're not there to greet her. Nuka's walks have a full agenda, from wildlife census to cleanup duty.

What the happiness experts say

It's clear that dogs find it hard to live their best lives if they don't get out for a walk pretty regularly. But what about people? We have all kinds of ways to get mental stimulation—we can read, watch videos, work, talk on the phone, and interact online. Why bother leaving the house?

Two things happen when you head out for an active break. First, you move your body, which most people don't do enough. Second, you free your mind to snap out of whatever it's been fixating on, which can boost both your mood and your productivity.

Happiness coach Kim Strobel says, "If you can just move your body for 30 minutes a day, it has this wonderful overall effect on you. It can be any form of movement, but when we move our bodies, the chemicals in our brains change. We get the serotonin hits, we get the dopamine hits, and then that chemical exchange has an overall effect on us for the rest of the day." Even though most people acknowledge that they feel better when they get out, many don't make it a priority. Strobel says, "How many of us stop after lunch and take a walk around the block? We think we don't have time for those things."

When you make time to get out and move, it's not wasted time. It's doing all kinds of good things for your body and your brain, including making you happier.

According to positive psychology research, not only can physical exercise help you create new brain cells, it can also have all these effects:

- Enhanced body image, self-esteem, and self-perceptions
- Improved sleep patterns
- Reduced emotional distress and increased well-being
- Reduced depression
- Reduced stress
- Increased general health

In fact, exercise is now commonly "prescribed" for people with anxiety and depression. And as I mentioned in "Shake it off," if you can go for your walk (or run, or ride) in a natural environment like a hiking trail or a park, the benefits are even greater. Researchers have found that people who go for walks in nature decrease their levels of anxiety, are better at preserving a positive mood, and even show improvements in their memory.

Although you may be reluctant to stop and go for a walk when you're extremely busy with work or dealing with other challenges, it might be the best way for you to make progress on a problem you're having trouble solving. Researchers tested people before and after going for a walk and found that after walking, the subjects scored higher on a number of creativity tests. Time away from your work has also been shown to increase productivity and help you recover from intense stress. Exercise, including walks, can give you the mental break you need to return to work refreshed and thinking more clearly.

> Early in my career, I had a job in downtown Toronto, in a building just a few blocks away from the shores of Lake Ontario. Whenever I could (especially if I was having a stressful day), I spent most of my lunch break walking down to the lake and back. I could only stay at the shore for a few minutes before it was time to turn around, but it was well worth it. Not only did I get all the benefits of going for a walk, but stopping to watch the water glistening and rippling for a few moments made me feel calm and peaceful. That little break would interrupt whatever pressures I'd been feeling all morning and give me a fresh start for the second half of my day.

How to be happier by going for a walk

What could be easier than stepping out of your house or workplace now and then? And yet, you might be struggling to do this on a regular basis. Have you been telling yourself that you don't have time to wander every day or exercise regularly?

In many ways, we've built a society that glamorizes being "busy" all the time, which leads to constant stress and, eventually, burnout. Doing something like going for a walk doesn't sound important or productive, so you may feel guilty about spending your time that way. But physical activity isn't the opposite of productivity, and we should stop thinking of it that way. You don't think of brushing your teeth as a waste of time. Brushing is preventive maintenance for your teeth—and walking is preventive maintenance for your happiness.

Walking doesn't actually need to be walking (and not everybody can walk, for any number of reasons). It can be any activity that gets you to take a break, preferably outdoors, and move your body.

Schedule the time

Start viewing physical activity as an essential part of your day. You can do this by literally adding it to your schedule. Put walks and other active commitments into your calendar. If you're waiting for your "spare time" to fit them in, they will not happen regularly. If you set aside time specifically for that purpose, you're much more likely to follow through.

Decide what times, days, and activities are most likely to work with your other commitments and will give you the best happiness return for your effort. There's no one right time to get outside and active; it depends on your lifestyle and your schedule. But don't talk yourself out of it by deciding there's no time available—you may need to look a bit closer and move some things around to make time.

Perhaps you're an early riser, or could be. Is there a bit of time before anyone else is up when you could take a walk or bike ride around the neighborhood? Or maybe you can go outside and do a bit of yoga in your yard. I'm a big fan of exercising in the morning because it ensures that I get my activity in before the day has a chance to get out of control. It also gives me a dopamine and endorphin boost that makes me feel good for the rest of the day.

What do you do on your lunch break at work? Go for a walk around the block or visit a nearby park *before* you sit down to eat. Or take your lunch with you and walk to a pleasant picnic spot when the weather is nice. Working through lunch might seem like it will get you ahead, but as the research shows, you need to take breaks to stay productive and solve problems. If you work straight through the day, you may actually be getting *less* accomplished.

Do you bring your kids to after-school activities like a sports practice or a class? Maybe you can start using the time while they're doing the activity to go for a walk, or even a run. Rather than sitting there watching and waiting, make the time work for you.

Be accountable to someone

If you have a dog, you're ahead of the game because your dog needs to go for walks anyway. Make it a priority to walk your dog yourself rather than counting on a dog walker or a family member to do it. Or make it a family activity to walk the dog together. Try to go on an enjoyable, energizing walk and keep the other things awaiting your attention out of your head. Don't rush through your dog walks, dragging your poor companion around the block. A dog's life is short; enjoy the time you have together.

If walking a dog isn't the answer for you, try to find someone else to keep you to your word. Maybe you have a neighbor who would enjoy being your walking buddy every morning, or a coworker who will get you out from behind your desk at lunchtime. You could also schedule family walks or date-night walks. If you want to do a more intense form of exercise, consider finding a workout buddy who will give you hell if you don't show up, or sign up for a class where people will ask what kept you away.

Accountability is one of the most effective ways to create a new habit and make it stick. If someone is counting on you, you won't want to let them down by canceling your plans. Letting yourself down, unfortunately, is much easier.

If you can't find someone to take part in your activities with you, a good alternative is to tell people what you're planning to do. Ask someone reliable to follow up with you and hold you to your word. Not wanting to explain to them why you didn't exercise will give you more incentive to stick to your plans. Telling them you did it will also give you a moment of pride and satisfaction, as well as approval from your accountability buddy. Ever wonder why runners love to tell everyone how far they ran? Try it yourself and you'll discover how good it feels. Doing your activity will make you happier, and as a bonus, you'll feel even better when you tell someone about it.

Paws and reflect

- Moving your body with any type of exercise will change the chemistry in your brain, allowing you to feel happier.
- Physical exercise also helps you create new brain cells, keeping your mind healthy.
- Going for a walk can be a great way to break out of a bad mood, or to release your mind to work on a problem without any pressure. Often, you will return to your task feeling more productive and creative.
- Schedule walks and other physical activities into your day, rather than trying to squeeze them in when you have "spare time."
- Find an accountability partner (or a dog) who will prevent you from skipping your activities when you are busy or don't feel like doing them.

Photo credit: Goran Horvat for Pixabay

10
Stop and smell things

Pawsitive dogma

Of all the gifts you can give, your attention is perhaps the greatest of all.

Note from Nuka

Smells tell me just about everything I need to know. I may not be able to read books like a human, but I can learn just as much by sniffing. My nose is a highly evolved tool that tells me all about the places and things around me. For me, going for a walk without stopping to smell stuff is like you going to an art gallery with the lights off—I don't get much out of it. Smelling helps me make sense of the world, feel like a part of it, and enjoy it. In other words, stopping to smell things makes me happy.

> People seem to have really useless noses. You walk into the kitchen and say, "Ooh, it smells like curry in here." You might as well read a book and say, "Ooh, it looks like English!" When I walk into the kitchen, it smells like ginger, ghee, onions, cumin, mustard seed, red chilis, chicken, tomato, coriander ... well, you get the idea. The details are what's interesting, if you stop to notice them.
>
> Humans don't notice much. You could be so much happier if you noticed all the amazing things around you every day. It's a beautiful world—you just have to sniff it in.

What the dog experts say

Smell is by far a dog's most dominant sense, and they have evolved to make the most of it. First of all, a dog has far more scent receptors than humans. We have around 5 million, while a beagle has around 225 million. It's hard to imagine the difference because it's so extreme. Dogs can sniff five or six times per second to gather as much information as possible. They even have an extra organ above the roof of their mouths for smelling; it's called the vomeronasal organ, and it lets them trap and process smells even more effectively.

What do dogs do with all this smelly data they gather? Their brains can analyze it in amazing detail. The part of a dog's brain that processes smells is proportionally 40 times larger than a human's. Something that takes up that much space must be important.

When a dog is out walking or at a park, they are taking in a massive amount of scent information. Every tree the local dogs visit becomes a kind of message board. As dog behavior experts like to say, the dogs leave each other "pee-mail" messages. According to anthrozoologist John Bradshaw, dogs likely memorize the scents of the dogs they meet. When they're checking out the scent marks on a tree, they find out if any of their friends have been there recently and catch up on some details left behind through pheromones and other chemicals. It might seem like your dog is sniffing at one spot for a ridiculously long time, but they are sorting out possibly dozens of urine marks that have accumulated over time from various dogs.

Even if your dog doesn't often get to socialize with other dogs (or isn't fond of socializing), by sniffing urine markings they can feel like part of the community. Letting your dog sniff helps them stay happy by giving them a chance to participate in the doggie social scene and decide whether to leave their own message behind.

Dog behavior expert and psychologist Alexandra Horowitz describes how the same walk around her New York City block is a fresh experience for her dog Finn every time, even though it looks exactly the same to her. "Each time I step out of my door, I see more or less the same block. No wonder Finn stops when we exit: it is a wholly new street, wearing odors of the six hours since we were last outside, waiting to be sniffed in."

Perhaps if we learn to stop and "sniff" things in our own way, we can also appreciate all the fresh, new things in our world every time we step out our front door. We just need to slow down and notice them, and give them a chance to bring back our sense of wonder, beauty, gratitude, and joy.

I'm always a little surprised to see Marlowe and Nuka sniff each other. They spend pretty much all their time together; what could they possibly learn from sniffing? But the more I learned about how dogs use smell to assess health, stress levels, and other detailed information, the more I realized that my dogs keep tabs on how their fur sibling is doing by regularly having a sniff. And when one of them has gone somewhere without the other (like the vet's office), the dog who stayed home has to thoroughly sniff the returning dog to discover what happened, who they were with, and whether it was a good or bad experience. Of course, there's also the muzzle sniff that tells them if the other dog found something delicious to eat and didn't share!

What the happiness experts say

Your brain receives around 11 million bits of sensory information every second, but you can only process around 40 bits per second. That's an amazing amount of stuff you need to filter out. You might say we've become a little too good at it. In fact, your mind is quite likely to be thinking of what you need to do later in the day instead of processing what's around you at any given moment.

How much do you remember about what you saw yesterday, or what you heard? What happened on your way to work or while you were walking your dog? Chances are, the details didn't really sink in. It's not surprising. There's a lot happening all around you, and not all of it is important. You need to choose what to focus your attention on.

When you aren't focusing on where you are and what's around you, you dismiss it as unimportant. As a result, you forget most of what happens during your routine activities. Horowitz remarks, "It is forgotten not because nothing of interest happens. It is forgotten because we failed to pay attention to the journey to begin with. On the phone, worrying over dinner, listening to others or to the to-do lists replaying in our own heads, we miss the possibility of being surprised by what is hidden in plain sight right in front of us."

How does this lack of attention affect your happiness? You are likely rushing through your day with goals and obligations in mind, rather than embracing the unplanned opportunities that might fall into your path. How many opportunities to make your day better have slipped away because your eyes were on your phone, or you didn't take the time to stop and take a closer look at something? You may not even take the time to appreciate or remember the pleasant things you do briefly notice, rushing on to the next thing before you can really enjoy them.

When you go somewhere new, say on a holiday, you probably pay a lot of attention to the details. Everything is unfamiliar, special, and worth noticing. Meeting new people can have the same effect. But as you grow used to things you stop giving them your attention. It's part of your brain's effort to filter out things that don't matter. Change could bring either opportunity or danger, so it's worth your attention. Anything else you dismiss as noise.

Happiness coach Kim Strobel works with her clients to bring their attention back to the everyday opportunities to find happiness. She says we should "really be able to savor and take in all of the senses. If I go for a walk, is my goal to do this walk around the block as fast as possible? Or am I strategically looking for things that I'm grateful for? Just like dogs, I stop and pay attention to things. I always try to let my dogs sniff and explore and be curious."

Strobel says that a curious attitude is a key ingredient in a happy life, and one that has gotten lost. "We're supposed to continue to be curious about the world, about our goals and what we want to experience—our growth. We can go through life on default, so life is just happening to us. When we're taking a walk or driving our car or spending time with someone or having dinner with someone, are we really immersed in the experience of it, using all our senses? Most of us aren't."

To fix this, you need to make an effort to pay attention to what's around you and become an active participant in your own life. Every sunrise or sunset, delicious smell in the kitchen, or quick chat with a friendly stranger is an opportunity to generate more happiness and feel better about the world you live in. Remember, your brain has a negativity bias, so to become happier you need to gather all the positive thoughts you can. You have to constantly seek out and notice the good things about your life.

I lived in New Zealand for seven years, in the coastal city of Wellington. If you've ever met anyone who has been to New Zealand, they've probably talked your ear off about how beautiful it is. As someone who grew up in a pretty flat place, being able to look across the harbor and see mountains was simply astounding to me. Even though I was a long-time resident, I never stopped feeling waves of gratitude for the beauty that surrounded me in my everyday life there. Standing at the edge of the harbor, I would say to myself, "I can't believe I actually get to *live* here!" It never got old. I never took it for granted. That's the gift I received from experiencing life as an immigrant. I wonder how many lifelong Wellingtonians regularly feel that same excitement about where they live?

How to be happier by stopping to smell things

We began to look at ways to take in what's happening around you in "Live in the moment." Let's expand on that by looking at three ways you can use your attention and your senses to capture more of the happy moments that happen every day.

1. Focus on the journey, not the destination.
2. Be open to serendipity.
3. Give the experience your full attention.

Focus on the journey, not the destination

If you're a goal-oriented person (which we're generally encouraged to be), it's easy to just push through whatever you're doing while you keep the final outcome in mind. Instead of thinking about the process of cooking dinner, you think about getting it on the table as soon as possible. Instead of focusing on how each exercise in your workout feels and how well you executed it, you just want to tick them off your program and hit the shower.

It takes an intentional shift in your attitude to focus on the journey, or the process, and make that as important as the outcome. But when you do this, you notice more details along the way, and you are likely to find the experience more gratifying and feel more positive about it. Almost any activity can be enhanced by treating it as worthy of your attention.

Happiness expert Stephanie Staples has a great example. For her, running in races is not about reaching the finish line faster than last time. She likes to participate, but she doesn't much care where she places or how fast she finishes, as long as she gets to the finish line "upright and smiling." The activity of running with others is what she enjoys about it. "I can chat with people along the way and go under the sprinklers and whoop up the crowd—it's all about the experience for me." When she crosses the finish line, there's no doubt that she'll think of the race in a positive way. If her time or placement were her only focus, she'd barely remember who or what she encountered on the course, and she'd only be happy if she met her outcome goals.

Be open to serendipity

Most people think of serendipity as simply a "happy coincidence," but it is actually more than that. The word was invented by Horace Walpole—a writer, historian, and politician in 18th-century England—who was captivated by the ancient Persian tale of the three princes of Serendip (a former name for what is now Sri Lanka). Here is Walpole's definition of serendipity: *a state of mind whereby a person, by good fortune and through awareness and sensitivity, frequently finds something better than that which he is seeking.*

You'll notice that the person has to be more than just lucky—they need to have "awareness and sensitivity" or the opportunity will probably go unnoticed. In the tale, each prince is searching for something and fails to find it, but each ends up finding something unexpected that is even more valuable to him.

If you think of your life as a set of goals that you either reach or fail to reach, you are setting yourself up for disappointment. Instead, keep your mind open and pay attention to the choices that present themselves at every stage of the journey. Perhaps you'll discover a new goal that will make you happier. Perhaps an opportunity you didn't know about will appear (and this may happen only after you fail to reach your original goal). Perhaps there's a better way to reach your goal than the path you carefully planned out. Few things in life are all-or-nothing if you keep your mind open to all the possibilities.

The lesson of serendipity is that if you become too focused on the outcome you're expecting or hoping for, you could miss out on something even better. Pay attention to all your options, even when you think you've already chosen one. Be open to changing your mind when circumstances change, if a new path might make you happier.

Give the experience your full attention

As I mentioned in "Live in the moment," you can make an experience matter to you more by savoring it. Let's look at how you can do that by stopping to smell things—and touch, see, taste, and listen to them.

Gathering more sensory information while you do something will focus your attention on it and give you a more profound experience. When you notice something, try to notice it with all of your senses. Perhaps you're out walking in the rain. Instead of speeding up and getting annoyed, pay attention to the sound the raindrops make hitting the ground, notice the change in the scent of the air, watch the ripples when the drops land in puddles, reach out from under your umbrella and feel the cool water on your hand. Make it a positive experience instead of an annoyance.

You likely pay more attention when things are going wrong. Counteract this by taking extra time to pay attention to the positive experiences in your day. As positive neuroplasticity expert Rick Hanson says, "Your attention is like a combination spotlight and vacuum cleaner: It highlights what it lands on and then sucks it into your brain—for better or worse."

What are those positive experiences anyway? Things that may seem neutral or routine can be turned into positive thoughts if you choose to see them that way. The sensation of writing your shopping list with a really smooth pen, the sky full of fluffy clouds, the pleasant chat you had with a stranger at the bus stop—these can all be positive experiences if you register them in your brain that way. You tell yourself stories all the time, and you can change the way you feel about an event by changing the story you tell about it. Positive psychologists call this "appreciative inquiry."

In fact, appreciation is one of the best ways to turn your efforts to stop and smell things into lasting positive emotions. Whenever you notice something good, take a moment to appreciate it and be grateful that you noticed it. Some people like to end each day by writing down all the things they feel grateful for in a gratitude journal. Others like to start the day this way, putting them in a grateful mindset and helping them see all the things they should be happy about as they go through their day.

Paws and reflect

- 🐾 People are excellent at filtering out information that doesn't seem important, but as a result you miss out on a lot of details and a lot of opportunities to let those things make you happier.
- 🐾 Staying curious about the world can help you become more aware of the good things you see, hear, touch, taste, and smell every day.
- 🐾 Try to enjoy the journey, experiencing all parts of your day fully, instead of focusing on your destination and ignoring the process of reaching it.
- 🐾 Stay open to different possibilities instead of rigidly sticking to your plans. Serendipity can bring you opportunities for happiness that you aren't expecting, but only if you are ready to embrace them.
- 🐾 You will have more positive thoughts and emotions if you make a point of enjoying the ordinary events and experiences you might otherwise take for granted.

Photo credit: Felix Wolf for Pixabay

11
Enjoy some treats

Pawsitive dogma

You cannot make yourself happy by denying yourself the very things that give you the most pleasure.

Message from Marlowe

Treats are the best! I love it when I get treats for doing a trick, or for staying calm when another dog walks past, or just because you have some bits left over from your dinner. I'm not worried about whether I did anything for the treat—I never turn down something good. When you're as awesome as I am, you deserve treats just because! And some of the best treats aren't even food. I love friendly visitors, belly rubs, chin scritches, trips to the beach—you name it.

Humans are kind of strange when it comes to treats. Sometimes you need to do something very specific before you "earn" a treat. Sometimes you think having a treat means you're not being strong. And then at other times, you eat all the treats at once and feel really bad about it. Treats are good. Everyone deserves treats. Even you!

What the dog experts say

When they're talking about dogs, people tend to use the word "treat" to mean some kind of food that isn't what the dog eats for their meals. Dog trainer Rachel Friedman defines a treat quite simply as "something your dog likes." She embellishes this with the Oxford dictionary definition of treat: *an event or item that is out of the ordinary and gives great pleasure.* When you expand your idea of a treat to fit these definitions, it's clear that your dog could consider any number of things to be a treat, and not all of them are edible. You might notice something else about both of these definitions—there's nothing in them that says treats need to be earned or deserved.

Friedman groups dog treats into three main categories: food, objects and toys, and interactions. Any food your dog likes that they don't always get can be a treat. Of course, not all food treats are created equal, so if you're using treats to reward an important behavior, you want to choose the stuff your dog is really excited about: chicken, cheese, peanut butter, or whatever they consider droolworthy.

Objects and toys are very individual, and one dog's prized possession might not even get a glance from another dog. But there are dogs with very strong play drives who think a toy is at least as good as a food treat. Lots of working dogs get toys as treats. For example, police dogs are usually rewarded with their favorite toy (anything from a ball to a rolled-up towel to a squeaky rubber chicken) when they complete a task. It works because it's fun for the dog, but also because the dog knows it means their handler is happy with them. That makes it a combination of toy and interaction—a double treat.

As for interactions, those are obviously most valuable when they involve the dog's favorite people (or dogs) and come with plenty of enthusiasm. An interactive treat could be as simple as saying "good dog" in a happy voice, it could involve pleasurable touch (stroking, scratches, cuddles, brushing, belly rubs, rough play, etc.), or it could include a whole experience (going for a walk or a hike, swimming, dock diving, playing fetch, playing chase, etc.).

This might seem like a lot of different treats. It is! That's one of the reasons dogs don't question whether they've earned their treat or had too many of them. They've simply accepted that treats can come your way many times every day, as long as you recognize them as treats.

> My husband and I decided we would not feed our dogs table scraps while we're in the dining room. They need to wait until we're finished eating (although Marlowe still gives us "armpit head" most nights, just to remind us to save something for him). If we have a few morsels left over for the dogs, we give those to them in the next room. They sit politely for their treats as soon as they realize the time has come. This is undoubtedly one of the highlights of their day, and I'm sure that when they smell their favorite foods cooking, like salmon, they are already anticipating an awesome treat later. They also enjoy getting crunchy treats like carrots and romaine lettuce or a "pupsicle" of frozen plain yogurt in the summer. Food doesn't need to be unhealthy to be a treat!

What the happiness experts say

Like dogs, we can enjoy a lot of different kinds of treats. Food is usually the first thing that comes to mind, but people also treat themselves to time off, a night out, a spa day, a new outfit or gadget, a tattoo, concert tickets, sleeping late, or a day (or week) at the beach. Anything you don't consider part of your everyday life is potentially a treat.

Unlike dogs, however, a lot of people believe they should only have treats when they've done something out of the ordinary to deserve them. People sometimes feel guilty about having treats, or turn down a treat when it's offered unexpectedly.

Some people even choose a treat they really want, and then make up a goal they need to achieve before they can get it. Happiness coach Kim Strobel says she calls out her clients for doing this. "I see this with women all the time. Women who are overweight who join a gym will say, 'I will buy myself nice workout clothes when I lose the weight.' And I say, you are worthy of nice workout clothes right now. It's not selfish to put yourself first. It's an act of self-love. I think this is a mentality—we give away, give away, give away—and we're only allowed to receive if certain things happen. But when we give to ourselves, in whatever form, it is an act of self-love."

You may have been told it's selfish to enjoy a lot of treats. That's only true if your enjoyment of a treat somehow deprives someone else of it. Generally, there are plenty of treats to go around, and many of them are in endless supply. For example, you can enjoy a day at the beach without depriving others of the opportunity to enjoy the beach. When you treat yourself to a manicure or a massage, you don't prevent others from having one; there are more appointments available. Your treat isn't selfish if it won't take one away from someone else. Even if there is a limited supply—say you ate the last cookie—who's to say you don't deserve it as much as anyone else?

Positive psychology expert Shawn Achor uses an old cliché to illustrate this point—the one where, presented with half a glass of water, optimists see the glass as half-full and pessimists see it as half-empty. Achor says, "Both optimists and pessimists are so focused on how to interpret the single glass in front of them, that they miss the fact that there is a third, equally true reality—a pitcher of water on the table to refill the glass." There are many ways to interpret the same situation. It's up to you to choose the interpretation that allows you to be happy, including the realization that there are enough treats available for everyone, including you.

Treats are often used as a reward for exercising self-control. You do this when you reward a dog for not jumping up on people or not barking, for example. You do it for yourself when you make little bargains like "If I go to the gym this morning I can get an ice cream later" or "When I lose 20 pounds I'm going to buy those jeans I like." There's a wonderful scene in the movie *Adaptation*, where Nicolas Cage, playing a struggling screenwriter, makes this kind of bargain while he stares at the blank page in his typewriter. He tells himself that if he comes up with some themes for his screenplay, he can deal with his hunger by getting a coffee and a muffin. He even decides on a muffin flavor (banana nut). Rather than just getting himself the treat so he can stop thinking about it, he uses it to try to force himself to focus on his work, and instead he becomes more and more focused on banana nut muffins.

You can get into trouble when you do too much of this bargaining and waiting. Self-control actually *is* in limited supply. Self-control researcher Roy Baumeister says that self-control is like a muscle that has to do work—there's only so much we can get it to do before it gets tired and stops functioning. Study subjects who worked really hard on self-control during one exercise were more likely to lose control and act impulsively during the next one. Denying yourself treats through self-control can backfire, because you get tired of holding back and end up overindulging in the next temptation. So instead of allowing yourself to have a cookie every now and then, you have no cookies at all for several weeks and then eat an entire package.

> I'm a big fan of cake—it's my number one treat. As you can imagine, a good cake is one of my favorite things about having a birthday. When my 50th birthday came around, I was trying to think of a fun way to mark the occasion—something that was totally "me." So I decided to have a cake party, where I told every guest they were expected to show up with a cake! Over the top? Perhaps, but it was a lot of fun and I enjoyed a little taste of almost everything. I had a stack of takeout containers ready so my guests could all take a selection of cake slices home with them, because even for me there would have been too much left over, and it would have stopped feeling like a treat. I certainly felt well celebrated and everyone had a great time. It was a super treat that turned an often-dreaded milestone into a memorable, happy event.

How to be happier by enjoying some treats

This might be a good time to repeat the definition of a treat: *an event or item that is out of the ordinary and gives great pleasure.* Your first step toward enjoying more treats—and enjoying your treats more—is to redefine which things in your life count as treats. Try to look at more of the good things in your life as treats. By recognizing more of them, they don't seem as decadent or selfish, which makes it easier to let them "give great pleasure" and make you happy.

For example, when it's watermelon season (which doesn't last for long here in Canada) I get very excited because I really enjoy eating sweet, juicy watermelon. By recognizing that watermelon is one of my treats, I get as much pleasure from eating it as I do from eating ice cream or another summery dessert. As a bonus, I don't need to fight the urge to feel guilty about having that treat because there are no negative consequences to eating watermelon (apart from sticky fingers).

Stop working for your treats

Change your approach to treats by not looking at them as something you either have or haven't "earned." This way of assessing treats can lead to treating yourself to stuff you don't really want that much, because you feel the need to reward yourself for reaching your goal. It can also lead to turning down a treat you'd really enjoy, because you feel like you didn't earn it.

What if, instead, you assessed treats as either "worth it" or "not worth it"? Choose the treats that will give you the most pleasure with the fewest downsides. How much would you enjoy the treat? When was the last time you had it? What other treat might you prefer? By selecting treats based on whether they are something you really want, and whether the pleasure you get from them outweighs any negative consequences of indulging, you can enjoy the treats that will make you happier and skip the ones that won't. This doesn't mean you can't have treats that are bad for you—just make sure they're really worth it to you!

Mix it up

Treats, by definition, can't be something you have every day. Otherwise, they cease to be treats and you start to take them for granted, feeling like you're actually being deprived if you don't get them. You may also feel guilty if you have the same treat all the time, because you know treats are meant to be occasional.

If you want your treats to give you more happiness, keep changing them. As social psychologist Jonathan Haidt says, "Variety is the spice of life because it is the natural enemy of adaptation." Perhaps trying something new can actually become the treat itself, whether it's a new food, a new activity, or a new social event. By keeping your treats fresh, you will enjoy them more instead of taking them for granted. And treats you enjoy more will make you happier.

Remember to enjoy it

Savoring (which we discussed in "Live in the moment") is another way to enjoy your treats more. Don't feel bad for indulging yourself; make the most of the experience so it feels worthwhile to you. Happiness and emotional intelligence expert Emma Seppälä suggests, "When you feel pleasure, close your eyes and be 100% present with that pleasure. Whether it is emotional (such as love) or sensual (food or touch or sound), savor the sensation or experience completely."

Psychology research has shown that when you savor or bask in something pleasurable, you extend that feeling of pleasure and feel more satisfied by it. If you totally immerse yourself in the enjoyment of eating a cookie, there's a much better chance you'll be happy with one or two of them and not try to fill a void in your happiness by consuming *all* the cookies.

It's easy to get caught in a trap where you feel bad about doing things that make you feel good. When you allow yourself to enjoy some treats, you open yourself up to experiencing those pleasures and positive thoughts without any guilt or negative thoughts to cancel them out.

Paws and reflect

- A treat is anything that is out of the ordinary and gives great pleasure. It doesn't need to be a reward for doing something specific.

- Using treats to reward your self-control can backfire because your self-control wears down and you will act more impulsively the next time you try to resist temptation.

- Try to view more of the pleasant things in your life as "treats" you occasionally enjoy. You will discover that treats are abundant and not necessarily bad for you.

- Instead of asking yourself whether you have or haven't "earned" a treat, ask whether or not you consider that particular treat "worth it" to you.
- Vary your treats so you don't start taking them for granted, at which point they will stop being treats.
- Savor your treats to get the most happiness from them. Practice feeling good, not guilty, about enjoying some treats.

Photo credit: Alexa for Pixabay

12
Accept praise

Pawsitive dogma

Allow people's praise and admiration to fill you up. When you push it away, it's an insult to both of you.

Message from Marlowe

Who's a good boy? I am! When my humans tell me I did something good or I'm beautiful or they're happy to see me, I believe them. Why wouldn't I? Their positive reinforcement makes me feel happy, safe, and loved.

I've noticed that some humans find it hard to accept praise or compliments. That's not very dog-like! Maybe you think you don't deserve it, or the person praising you is just trying to make you feel better—worse still, some of you might even think it's a trick to get something from you.

When someone tells you that you look nice or did a good job, it can make you happy all day long. But first you need to believe it.

What the dog experts say

Dogs enjoy our praise because we've bred that response into them. Over thousands of years, humans have selectively bred dogs who are eager to please us. This was important when most dogs had jobs, like guarding livestock or helping with a hunt. If dogs didn't care what their people wanted, they would run off with the prey after a hunt and eat it themselves. So we kept breeding the dogs who cared. Today, dogs pay a lot of attention to their humans, including whether we seem happy about what they're doing.

Studies at the Duke Canine Cognition Center found you can predict who will be the "smartest" dogs (who perform best at tests) by selecting the friendliest dogs. The dogs who have evolved to cope best in our human world are the ones who are the most tuned in to what we think and expect from them. And one of the ways dogs have learned what we expect is by paying attention to our praise and seeking the satisfaction it gives them.

Positive reinforcement training for dogs usually involves rewarding a new trick or behavior with food treats, and then gradually replacing the treats with praise. It's kind of amazing that dogs like our approval so much that they're happy to continue doing what we ask after we stop giving them food for it, as long as they keep getting praise.

Dogs learn to associate certain words with approval (like "good dog"), but the praiser's tone of voice is even more important. High pitch and enthusiasm tell a dog they've done well—it's the same tone we use to praise and encourage babies.

Dog trainer Nicole Barnett says, "Praise and happy talk are a great way to prompt behavior. Dogs are intrigued when we make happy, silly sounds." She adds that dogs are much better at noticing mixed signals than humans are. You might not notice that when a colleague in a meeting says you've asked a great question, their body language suggests they are actually annoyed with you. Barnett says, "Dogs can decipher when we're happy or sad or angry. They have an amazing ability to pick up on our body language and our communication skills. I think dogs are way better at picking up on our body language than we are with theirs."

Marlowe's face tells me everything I need to know about the power of praise. When he's focused on something his ears are perked up, his brow furrowed, and his gaze intense. His mouth may be closed as he sniffs at something or concentrates. If I praise him for what he's doing (or what he just did) his whole demeanor changes. The ears relax and lie flat and back on his head, his eyes soften, and his mouth drops open and relaxes into a doggie smile. This is a dog who is super proud to be a good boy!

What the happiness experts say

Many people are uncomfortable with getting compliments or praise. When someone says they like your hair or your smile, do you immediately say something negative about yourself? Your reaction comes down to your feelings of self-esteem or self-worth. If you don't think you're worthy of praise, it can be hard to accept it gracefully.

Happiness coach Kim Strobel says, "We will actually shove compliments away. And every time we push away a compliment or a blessing or a kindness, what we're inadvertently doing is telling the universe we're not worthy of receiving that gift that someone wants to bestow on us. I always tell people, the root of most of our problems is self-love. Why is it that we don't deem ourselves worthy of receiving a kind gesture from someone?"

The difficulty some people have in accepting praise may be taught to them as children. Kids are often told to be modest or humble and to not brag about themselves, but we can take that too far. Social welfare expert Katherine Compitus says that humility often crosses the line into low self-esteem. "We think we're being humble by putting ourselves down. I don't think that's healthy. I think that we should enjoy a compliment. Self-love is healthy. We should not be scared to like ourselves."

In addition to being taught to be humble, you may have been told you need to work hard if you want to achieve great things. That can make you very self-critical when you feel you aren't meeting the high (maybe impossibly high) expectations you've set for yourself, even if other people tell you you're doing really well. Harsh self-criticism is actually quite destructive, and it doesn't help you achieve more. Instead, it backfires and makes you feel like you are not good enough and won't ever amount to anything. Eventually, you may lose the will to keep trying.

Fitness expert Oonagh Duncan sees again and again how being hard on yourself can backfire when it comes to weight loss and fitness. She says, "Negative, self-hating thoughts will lead to negative, self-hating behavior. There is no other outcome. No one ever *hated* themselves into a body they loved. That has never happened." Instead, she urges her clients to love who they are right from the beginning of their fitness journey. Self-love shouldn't be dependent on reaching your goals.

And while you tend to exaggerate your faults, you may fail to notice all your positive traits. Instead, you probably take them for granted and consider them no big deal. When someone else notices one of these things and compliments you on it, you might feel it's not worthy of a compliment because you simply expect it of yourself. Take a moment to realize it was worthy enough that someone else not only noticed it but went out of their way to mention it to you. Maybe it's a bigger deal than you think.

I've discovered the power of unexpected compliments, and I think they're even more powerful when they come from a total stranger—someone who has nothing to gain from saying something nice to you and no obligation to do so. The first one I remember giving was at a work-related social event. Another company was having an event at the same place and I saw a woman with curly hair like mine. She had a really nice hairstyle and I asked if I could take a picture of her to show to my hairstylist. She blushed and seemed really surprised, but she agreed and I could see it made her feel beautiful. It also made me feel good to praise someone honestly and add some happiness to her day. I've since made a point of telling total strangers that a particular color looks great on them, they have excellent form when they swim, and other little (and always true!) compliments. It's a simple thing to do, but I wouldn't be surprised to find out that those few kind words stayed with them for the rest of the day and made them feel genuinely better about themselves.

How to be happier by accepting praise

If you respond more strongly to criticism than you do to praise, you're not alone. It's part of the negativity bias in your brain to respond to bad news more strongly than good news. For example, if you've just had an annual review at work and your manager said you were doing five things well and one thing needed improvement, you probably ignored the five good things and left feeling upset about the one you were criticized for.

Learning to accept praise is important for your happiness because it reinforces positive feelings about yourself. It also encourages you to keep working hard toward achieving your goals because the effort is paying off.

Stop rejecting praise

Changing how you respond to praise will take time and practice, just like everything else. Happiness coach Kim Strobel recommends "letting yourself feel uncomfortable, but changing your response. It's retraining yourself to say, 'As uncomfortable as this feels, I'm going to look the person in the eyes and say thank you.'" The next time someone gives you a compliment, thank them without saying anything critical about yourself. Fight the urge to downplay what they said. If it helps you, say something nice about them in return.

According to happiness expert Stephanie Staples, you shouldn't waste these opportunities to let other people make you happy. "Someone's giving you something on a silver platter. Here it is, the universe is offering this to you—an opportunity, a compliment—on a silver platter. And if you don't receive it graciously, it's like you're just flipping that platter away, saying I don't want that. I think we need to accept it graciously and know that we're worthy of it and that we deserve it."

Practice on yourself

You can also practice praising yourself to boost your self-esteem and cancel out some of your excessive self-criticism. Duncan encourages her clients to practice feeling sexy, confident, and happy right from the start—long before they've reached their fitness goals. Do those jeans make your booty look great? Strike a pose in the mirror! Just like when you're training a muscle to do something new, you might feel weak and clumsy praising yourself at first, but you will get better at it over time and it will take less effort.

Giving yourself compliments opens you up to accepting compliments from others, because you train your brain to believe you deserve them. Think about what you're good at. Maybe it's supporting your friends, organizing events, raising money for charity, or playing Scrabble. Whatever you do well, recognize that you truly have this talent or skill and that it matters. Own your positive qualities and let them be a source of pride and happiness for you. When you embrace being good at something, it becomes a pleasant experience when someone else comments on it instead of an awkward one.

Praise others

You might find that giving compliments is your gateway to learning to accept them. If that's where you need to begin, get started right away with friends, family members, work colleagues, and even total strangers. Aim to eventually start accepting compliments as enthusiastically as you give them, and truly believe you have talents and qualities that are special and worthy of admiration.

If you still feel uncomfortable accepting praise, think about this: humans are hardwired for reciprocity—we believe in a fair exchange. Almost every religion in the world has some version of the "golden rule": treat other people the way you would like to be treated. The more positivity you put out into the world, the more you're likely to get back. It's another step on the road to happiness.

How does it feel when you give someone a heartfelt compliment and they brush it off or respond with self-criticism? It's awkward for you because you sincerely wanted to say something nice and make them happy, but instead you seem to have upset them. Remember that feeling when someone compliments you. If you accept the compliment and thank them for it, they will feel good about giving it. Being kind and generous gives you positive feelings, so compliments that are well received make *both* people happier.

Paws and reflect

- If you struggle to accept praise without putting yourself down, you may need to build up your self-esteem.
- You will achieve more of your goals by accepting encouragement and being happy in your current state than you will by criticizing yourself and feeling you aren't good enough to be worthy of praise.
- Practice accepting people's compliments and praise graciously. Learning to accept praise can help you feel more satisfied with your life.
- Positive self-talk can raise your self-esteem and make it easier for you to accept praise from other people.
- Try to praise and compliment others more often. It will make both of you feel good, as well as normalize the idea that praise is genuine and deserved.

Photo credit: Ian Lindsay for Pixabay

13
Play fetch

Pawsitive dogma

Putting in the effort to get the things you want can actually feel more satisfying than having them.

Note from Nuka

Playing fetch is fun! First of all, I get to chase something—and I just love chasing things. Then I get excited when I catch it. Then when I bring it back to my human I get praise and sometimes even a treat, which is awesome too. And then I get to do it all over again.

Humans don't play fetch the same way dogs do, but I've noticed you have your own versions. Sometimes you fetch new clothing or books or electronic gadgets, even if you already have lots. Sometimes you solve a puzzle, and as soon as you finish you start another. Just like holding on to the ball is only fun for a moment, getting whatever thing you wanted is only fun for a moment, and then you need to start the chase again.

What the dog experts say

People have trained their dogs to fetch for centuries. Most dogs can learn the game because it's based on a natural system their ancestors used when they lived in cooperative packs. When some members of the pack went out hunting, they brought back some of their prey to the den to share. Without a system like this, the pups would starve and so would pack members left behind to guard the pups, as well as any pack member who was injured or sick and couldn't participate in the hunt.

Humans adapted this behavior to suit our own hunting needs. Dogs were trained to fetch small prey (like birds or rabbits) after it was killed and bring it back to the hunters. In return for their help, the dog would be fed and protected by the humans.

Over time, we've created strong fetching instincts through selective breeding in certain dogs and labeled them as "retrievers." Dog behavior expert Stanley Coren told me about a flat-coated retriever he once had who loved to fetch. He tried testing to see how many times the dog would fetch the same toy, but after 91 throws Coren had to give up because his arm was too sore. Clearly, his dog was born to fetch.

13. PLAY FETCH

The thrill of the chase is also part of a dog's hunting instincts. When prey runs away, dogs get the urge to run after it. You can trigger the same response by throwing a ball or a stick and watching your dog take off in pursuit.

Some dogs quickly lose interest in fetching, though. A new toy might get them interested for a while, since new things are more valuable than stuff they already own. Some dogs will change the rules after a while to keep the game interesting—for instance, a dog might switch from traditional fetch to a game of "keep-away," where they try to stop you from getting the toy and hope you'll chase them around.

> Neither of our dogs will spend long playing fetch, but Nuka does like the chasing part. She loves chasing snowballs in the winter. When there's been a big snowfall, I will make a fist-sized snowball and toss it across the yard, where it will fall into the snow and leave an entry hole. Nuka bounds across the yard to the place where it disappeared and shoves her face into the snow to find it. Half the time, the snowball breaks apart when it hits the ground, so there's nothing to find. It must be a big mystery to Nuka when there's nothing there. Even when she can locate the snowball, it usually falls apart when she tries to pick it up. But she's happy to chase after the next one all the same.

What the happiness experts say

People also love the thrill of the chase, but for us it can be a double-edged sword. On the positive side, becoming deeply involved in a pursuit is inherently satisfying, and you can become much better at things when you enjoy practicing them again and again. On the negative side, you can become convinced that the pursuit of something new is always better than enjoying what you already have. Whether it's a new job, a new romance, or a new pair of shoes, when you are sure there's always something better out there to find, you can create unhealthy behavior patterns that can leave you unsatisfied with your life and even destroy your relationships. If your closet is full of never-worn clothing or you have shelves and shelves of unread books, this means you!

Let's start with the positive way to play fetch. Positive psychology pioneer Mihaly Csikszentmihalyi was interested in the way painters sometimes became so engaged in their work that they didn't notice that they hadn't eaten all day or they'd been holding up their arm in an awkward way for hours. This inspired Csikszentmihalyi's research on what he later called "flow," where you become so immersed in what you're doing that you lose track of time, and the activity itself is even more rewarding than the result at the end. For example, a rock climber might climb the same rock face over and over again (playing "fetch" with reaching the top of the climb) and always enjoy it, even though their goal has already been reached many times. The flow they feel during the activity is what they enjoy, rather than the result. Csikszentmihalyi interviewed artists, mountain climbers, chess players, surgeons, writers, and manual laborers who did what they did for the sheer love of it.

The old cliché—do what you love and you'll never work a day in your life—might actually be true if your job puts you in a state of flow. Sometimes doing the same work every day doesn't really feel like work because doing it makes you feel a sense of mastery and accomplishment, and the days fly by as you stay absorbed in your favorite activity. Unfortunately, few jobs allow people to stay in a state of flow all day. Most jobs include tasks that are less satisfying.

Neuroscience confirms that the satisfaction you get from doing something challenging is actually longer lasting and deeper than the satisfaction that comes after you accomplish it. Psychology researcher Richard Davidson calls the positive feelings you have when you're making progress toward a goal the "pre-attainment positive affect." This is the excitement you feel when you can see you're making progress, you feel like things are going well, and you really start to believe in yourself and your ability to reach your goal.

When you reach your goal, your brain goes through a different reward process called the "post-attainment positive affect." That stage is more a feeling of contentment rather than excitement. It slips away much faster than the thrill you felt while you were working toward your goal. Once you hit your goal, it doesn't take long to revert to your baseline level of happiness.

The downside of playing fetch comes when you find yourself chasing that fleeting moment of pleasure from reaching the goal or getting something new. Fitness expert Oonagh Duncan says that people often confuse pleasure with happiness, but they aren't the same thing. "Pleasure is a momentary feeling that comes from some external source. Happiness, on the other hand, is internal and long lasting. The problem arises when pleasure comes at the cost of happiness." For example, eating donuts might give you pleasure but not happiness. When you keep going after the short-term pleasure you get from eating another donut, you might actually be working against the better health and higher self-esteem that will bring you lasting happiness.

Positive psychology expert Bridget Grenville-Cleave says, "We adapt, we get used to things, whether it's the things we buy or other positive events and experiences in our lives. When that happens, we start taking them for granted, quickly reverting to our usual happiness baseline. This is what happens when 'the novelty wears off.'" Psychologists refer to this constant search for the next new, pleasurable thing the "hedonic treadmill." Because it only works when the new thing is new, you're constantly looking for your next hit of pleasure. To find real happiness, you need to get off the treadmill.

I've already mentioned my love of cake, but I don't just enjoy eating cake—I also love to bake. I started baking as a young girl. When I asked my mother for a lightbulb-powered toy oven to bake mini-cakes, her response was, "Why don't you use the real oven and bake enough for all of us?" So she taught me to bake cakes and cookies and to cook various meals, and as I grew older I tried more and more recipes and techniques. For me, baking and cooking are inherently rewarding because you end up with something you can enjoy, and you can continually experiment and improve your results. You're never "done" cooking and baking, because you eat every day. And there's always something new and challenging to try, so it doesn't get boring. Cooking and baking are definitely my favorite way to play fetch.

How to be happier by playing fetch

The key to using a game of fetch to improve your happiness is to embrace the positive version of fetch (flow) and avoid the negative version (the hedonic treadmill). To do this, it's important to think of fetch as a game where the fun part is the activity itself (running after the ball), not the goal (having the ball).

Find your flow

First, think about what activities you enjoy the most. Is there anything you do that puts you in that state of flow, where you are so immersed in what you're doing that you lose track of time and don't even notice what else is going on? It could be just about anything: crossword puzzles, knitting, fixing things, playing an instrument, weight training, carpentry—you name it. It should be something you find challenging, because otherwise you won't become immersed. Of course, this activity should ideally be something that has a positive effect. You don't want to become fully immersed in starting bar fights, for example.

If you can't think of anything that puts you in this state, maybe it's time to take up a new activity you're interested in but haven't had a chance to try yet. Or you can think of things you used to do but stopped because you didn't have time for them or you no longer see the people who did them with you. Perhaps you used to love sailing but you don't have a boat. Could you join someone else's crew or get a small boat? Maybe you enjoyed drawing as a kid but haven't done it since high school. Buy a sketchbook and find out if it still holds your attention. Take a drawing class to rekindle your feelings of accomplishment.

Change your perspective

If you enjoy doing things that could potentially lead you down the negative, goal-chasing path, try to change the way you look at them. Take the emphasis off the goal and put it on the process. Just because you enjoy shopping with your friends doesn't mean you have to go into debt from constantly buying stuff you don't need.

Social welfare expert Katherine Compitus says it's all in your perspective. "We can enjoy going shopping with our friends—and it's the going with friends that we enjoy, it's the journey. That's what we can learn from dogs in that situation. That they enjoy the journey, while we're always looking for the destination. And the destination never is good enough for us; it's a moving target. So I think we have to take a moment and be grateful that we have the time to go shopping, that we have somebody to go shopping with, or that we enjoy spending time by ourselves. When we stop expecting and start appreciating, that's when we turn our perspective that little bit. Then we can see that it's the journey, not the destination, that fulfills us."

You can also change your perspective on the things in your life that are not new, but that can give you positive experiences if you take the time to look at them with fresh eyes. Your brain is quite flexible this way, and you can get it to react like it does to getting something new by making an old thing new again.

If eating out with your partner feels like just another meal, start thinking of it as "date night" to make it an event worth enjoying. When you're on the couch relaxing with your dog, feel the softness of the fur on their ears and look into their big puppy dog eyes. This type of renewed experience gives your brain a dopamine hit that makes you feel happier.

By focusing on the pleasant experiences you have, and being satisfied with the good things that are already part of your life, you can find ongoing happiness in the things you enjoy doing without getting on that hedonic treadmill, where what you have is never good enough. Positive neuroplasticity expert Rick Hanson says you should focus on taking in and truly cherishing the pleasure of the positive things in your life. "If you do this regularly, you'll feel already full, with no reason to chase after or grab on to pleasant experiences."

Paws and reflect

- 🐾 The key to playing "fetch" is to find joy in the activity itself instead of being happy only when you reach your goal.
- 🐾 The best activities are ones that put you in a state of flow, where you're completely engaged in what you're doing and feel satisfied whenever you do it.
- 🐾 It's important to avoid the "hedonic treadmill," where you seek out new things and then get tired of them quickly, so you need to keep replacing them with something newer.

🐾 Look at the things you already have in your life with new eyes. You can keep appreciating the friends, possessions, surroundings, and activities that make you happy as long as you never take them for granted.

Photo credit: Katryn B. for Pixabay

14
Chase the uncatchable

Pawsitive dogma

How can you know what's possible until you try to achieve the impossible? Chase the sky and you may discover you can fly after all.

Message from Marlowe

I know there are things I'm not supposed to chase, but I just can't help it. I see that squirrel on the fence mocking me, and I just have to run after it. The darn thing never falls off the fence, but I keep on chasing it anyway. One of these days I might just catch it. I got pretty close last time!

People like chasing stuff too, but usually not squirrels. Instead, you chase things like fame, wealth, or physical perfection—stuff that sounds a lot harder to catch than a squirrel, if you ask me. You probably won't get that stuff, so why chase after it? Maybe people actually enjoy chasing as much as dogs do.

What the dog experts say

Many dogs still have powerful hunting instincts, even though few of them need to catch their own meals these days. Their prey drive kicks in automatically when they see something speeding away from them. That could include squirrels, cats, rabbits, raccoons, and (unfortunately) skunks and porcupines. It could also include cars, skateboards, bicycles, and, in some cases, the dog's own tail. Dogs that have been bred to chase, like greyhounds, have a stronger urge to run after fast targets. Herding dogs, on the other hand, might actually be trying to round up the neighborhood cats or kids—or even the cars.

As I pointed out in "Play fetch," the thrill of the chase is satisfying in itself for dogs, so catching isn't their only motivation. But to make the chase fun, there probably needs to be at least a minuscule chance (at least in their minds) that the prey could be caught.

For some dogs, the point of the chase is not to catch the animal or object, but to chase it away. A dog that runs after a car might be trying to protect their family or their property from it. The fact that the car speeds off reinforces the behavior by making the dog feel like they've accomplished their goal—the car ran away.

Unfortunately, this chasing instinct, whatever its motivation, can get dogs into a lot of trouble. I know of at least two dogs who have chased something onto nearby train tracks in our neighborhood and been struck and killed by a train. There are also dogs who never seem to learn that it ends badly when they chase a skunk (sadly, Marlowe is one of them).

But most of the time, chasing the uncatchable gives dogs a boost in energy and some mental stimulation. Dogs are happier when they have a job to do and they feel like they're doing it well. You could consider it a dog's version of flow, where an activity becomes all-consuming and feels satisfying while they're doing it. It's up to humans to make sure chasing happens in a safe way (for both dogs and prey). It's not inherently a bad thing for them to try to catch something uncatchable, and to keep trying even though they always fail.

> One day I was working at my computer, and I could hear Marlowe outside barking and barking. It was going on for a long time, so I went out to see what was happening. It turned out there were a couple of crows in our neighbor's tree and Marlowe was having a rather loud argument with them. Yes, they were shouting back at him! Marlowe doesn't like crows and will chase them whenever he sees them. The fact that the crows in the tree were completely out of reach didn't stop him from trying to chase them away by barking. Whenever he sees a crow by the side of the road, he'll try to run after it. He must know they can fly and he can't, but he wants to chase after them anyway. I always warn him, "Don't mess with the crows, Marlowe. They're smarter than you!" So far they haven't plotted revenge against him, as far as I know, but he should probably watch his back.

What the happiness experts say

People also like to chase things that are hard to catch—but we like to call them "goals" or "dreams." What's the difference between a goal and a dream? Your perceived likelihood of success. A goal is something you believe you can achieve one day if you keep working hard at it. A dream is something you don't necessarily think will ever happen, but you strongly believe that achieving it would make you very happy. Even if your dreams are not very realistic, chasing after them, especially if you appreciate the progress you're making along the way, can make you happier.

Positive psychology expert Shawn Achor defines happiness as "the joy we feel moving toward our potential." Without a goal or a dream, there's no incentive to move forward and find out how much potential you truly have. Not all goals are "uncatchable," so you can find happiness without chasing something that falls into that category. However, big dreams can be powerful motivators.

Achor studied people who were living in identical circumstances and tried to understand why some were thriving while others felt completely hopeless. What it came down to was their own perception of reality. Those who were happy and thriving lived in a mental world where achieving things was possible, despite the obstacles they faced. The others didn't see the possibilities and gave up any hope that they could improve their lives. This means, to some extent, you create your own reality and it can make you either happier or less happy, depending on the kind of world you decide you're living in. Achor says, "Before we can be happy and successful, we need to create a positive reality that allows us to see the possibility for both."

Pursuing a big dream gives you a reason to work hard. Emotional intelligence expert Emma Seppälä says that we value things more if we worked hard to get them. If you want to start your own company, for example, you might dream of having it valued at a billion dollars one day. If you want to be an actor, perhaps your dream is to win an Academy Award or an Emmy. If you take up running, your dream may be to win the Boston Marathon or an Olympic gold medal. Very few people achieve such dreams, but they dream of them nonetheless.

Social welfare expert Katherine Compitus says that having big dreams helps increase your self-esteem. "One of the secrets of highly successful people is that when you aim high, you work toward that high. But it also means you hold yourself in high regard. Believing in yourself is very healthy and very good. Somebody who has those high goals, who is driven, will say, 'Just because I didn't get this one thing, it doesn't mean I can't achieve this other thing.' Every setback is motivation to move even further forward. It's a learning experience rather than an opportunity to fall apart."

The biggest problem with chasing the uncatchable is when you tie your self-worth to reaching that nearly impossible goal, and you don't see how much you've achieved along the way. Happiness coach Kim Strobel warns that the goalposts often move. When you reach a goal you set for yourself, you are satisfied for a moment and then start to take it for granted. Then you set a higher goal—and you may feel like a failure again until you reach it. Instead, it's important to celebrate those incremental wins and stay aware of how far you've come.

Strobel also stresses that you shouldn't forget about the other good parts of your life while you're pursuing your dream. "You need to be able to find your happy in the now—right now—even if you haven't attained your goals. It's so important that we look around us and say, 'What are the things I have right now, so that I can be happy while I continue to chase those goals and dreams.'"

> It may not surprise you to hear that my childhood dream was to become a writer. In my mind, that meant writing novels and having them published. After several unimpressive attempts, I realized I was not at all talented at writing fiction. It wasn't until I redefined my dream that I found a way to make it a reality. I may not have a bestselling novel in me, but I can write helpful and fun nonfiction books! My first concept caught the interest of an agent, and he landed me a contract with a small publisher. I achieved my dream of becoming a published author with *Sex in a Tent*! It took a couple of decades and a lot of steps along the way, but keeping an open mind and learning about my strengths and weaknesses as I progressed made the journey and the hard work worthwhile. And seeing my name on the cover of a book definitely made me happy. If I'd been completely discouraged because I couldn't achieve my dream of being a novelist, I'd probably have given up entirely. Instead, here I am releasing my fourth nonfiction book.

How to be happier by chasing the uncatchable

The trick to chasing the uncatchable is to use your goals and dreams to make you happier instead of feeling overwhelmed with disappointment because you may not ever achieve them. If you deny yourself happiness until you win a Nobel Prize or make the Olympic team, you'll miss the opportunity to enjoy your experiences and achievements as you chase the dream.

Choose the right thing to chase

The first step is to identify your goal or dream. What would be so amazing that you're willing to work toward achieving it for years? It could be a career goal or a personal goal, as long as it's important to you.

Happiness expert Stephanie Staples says that choosing your own definition of success makes it available to anyone, not just a few high achievers. "I believe 'success' is for everybody. It's not just for people who were born on this side of the tracks or people who had this amount of education—it's not just for a certain number of people. Everybody deserves and can have whatever *their version* of success is."

One thing to watch for as you decide what to chase is to make sure it's a goal you can work *toward* (an "approach goal"), not a goal to *avoid* something (an "avoidance goal"). Focusing on avoidance goals (like not gaining weight or not losing your job) doesn't actually help you feel happier. According to positive psychology expert Bridget Grenville-Cleave, approach goals are good for you "firstly because making progress towards achieving a valued goal makes us feel good, and secondly because we get a sense of satisfaction from identifying and pursuing life goals which are consistent with our core values." Avoidance goals fail to do this for us because, according to Grenville-Cleave, "constantly monitoring negative possibilities drains our energy and enjoyment, eventually taking its toll on our well-being. Even when they are successfully achieved, they can only ever lead to the *absence* of something negative."

Once you find a dream or goal you're excited about, you need to determine what steps will move you in the right direction as you chase it. What skills do you need to learn? What experience do you need to accumulate? Whose help and support will you need? What are the milestones you can achieve along the way that will let you know you're on the right track? Having a plan for achieving your goal dramatically increases your chances of ever reaching it. On the flip side, focusing on the ways your plan might fail can kill your motivation and lead to those very failures. And as we discussed in "Stop and smell things," staying too attached to the details of your plan can blind you to new and better possibilities that might emerge through serendipity.

Track your progress

When you're chasing a big dream or life goal, it's important to recognize how far along the path you've already come, rather than only looking at how far you still have to go. When all you see is the seemingly endless road ahead, it's easy to lose motivation and feel hopeless. But if you make a point of appreciating everything you've accomplished so far, you'll feel much more satisfied with how things are going and be motivated to continue working hard.

Try keeping a goal journal, where you write down everything you've done toward reaching your goal, and how you're feeling about your progress. This can help when you feel like you aren't getting any closer to success. Looking back through your journal, you'll see how much you've already accomplished.

Achor suggests starting each day by asking yourself what action you are going to take that day that will move you closer to your goal. By thinking about it intentionally every day, you train your brain to recognize that you are moving forward and you remind yourself to make your dreams a priority in your life. Even if you take the same action every day (for example, "I'm going to write another 1,000 words of my bestselling book"), this practice will remind you that every step you take is meaningful.

Any time it looks like you're getting close to one of your milestones (or even your big goal), take notice of the fact that you are about to score a big win. When you really believe a goal is reachable, your brain releases chemicals that supercharge your motivation, making you even more likely to get there soon. Achor says, "No matter what your goal is—whether it's finishing the marathon, completing a big project at work, or losing twenty pounds—your brain behaves in the exact same way. As soon as your brain registers that you are going to achieve your goal, it releases these same chemicals that give you the extra boost you need to accelerate." Once the finish line is in sight, you can sprint toward it and raise your arms in victory.

What if you never achieve your big dream? As long as you choose the right dream to chase, everything you do while pursuing it will add more happiness to your life. Keep enjoying the thrill of the chase, the small wins along the way, and the sense of accomplishment from looking back at everything you've already done.

Paws and reflect

- 🐾 Choose a dream that's so important to you that you're willing to work toward it for years. You need to pursue *your* dream, not anyone else's.

- 🐾 If you don't have an ambitious goal and dream, you might not be motivated to spend much time on the things that are most important to you.

- 🐾 It's important not to tie your self-worth to accomplishing your ultimate goal. You need to love yourself as you are, not as you imagine you will be after reaching your goal.

- 🐾 Make a plan to get you closer to your dream, and keep track of your progress. Be sure to reflect on how far you've come, celebrate every milestone, and enjoy the journey.

- 🐾 Even if you never achieve your dream, chasing it can make you happier and boost your self-esteem, as long as you recognize your progress along the way.

Photo credit: Stacey McDowall "Mimi"

15
Curl up and sleep

Pawsitive dogma

Sleep is your time for healing, rejuvenating, learning, de-stressing, understanding, and problem-solving. You wake up a better person after a good sleep.

Message from Marlowe

Sleep is really important stuff. I need my rest overnight so I can be alert and ready for action at the break of dawn. But one sleep isn't quite enough. A nice nap during the day on my comfy pillow and a lazy evening snoozing near my people also make me happy.

People seem to feel bad about sleeping. It's like the time you spend sleeping doesn't count for anything. But you need lots of sleep if you want to have a healthy and happy life. And it feels good too! I think it's time to take another look at sleep and realize it's one of the most important things you do every day.

What the dog experts say

If your dog appears to sleep a lot, you're not imagining it. Dogs sleep, on average, for close to half the day, or 10 to 12 hours. It varies from dog to dog, of course, and working dogs generally don't get as much "down time" as companion dogs for napping during the day.

Dogs need sleep for the same basic reasons as people: sleep supports their immune system, brain function, ability to learn, and retention of memories. It also helps them recover from negative or upsetting experiences. And just like people, dogs who don't get enough sleep tend to get stressed out and grumpy!

If you watch dogs sleep, it's clear that they go through periods where they are dreaming, just like humans. Dogs dream about their usual activities, and possibly replay some of the day's experiences. Researchers discovered this by temporarily blocking the brain function that partly paralyzes dogs (and humans) in their sleep. Without that usual limitation, the dogs could act out their dreams completely. They observed the dogs doing activities that were typical for them. For example, pointers actually stalked and pointed in their dreams, as though they were out hunting.

Your dreaming dog may move their legs (chasing something), whimper (barking or whining), smack their lips (eating), or move their tail (wagging). Dogs that have just been through an emotional event spend more time in REM sleep, which is associated with dreaming and consolidating memories. If you've ever slept for an unusually long time after an emotionally difficult experience, you were probably processing your experience the same way dogs do.

Dogs are crepuscular, which means they're most active around sunrise and sunset. Back when their ancestors had to hunt for their meals, those were the times when it was easiest to find prey at watering holes and other locations. Although most dogs don't need to hunt these days, those internal schedules have stuck around. The same instincts that tell them to get up early also tell them to have a snooze during the middle of the day. Historically, midday napping gave them a chance to digest anything they killed and ate in the morning, kept them out of the hot sun, and preserved their energy for another hunt at dusk.

Today's nonworking dogs likely sleep more than they really need to, mainly because they are left alone for long periods during the day and, frankly, there's not much else to do. But they don't usually sleep for long periods of time. Dogs tend to doze off for 45 minutes or so, then wake up for a bit to see what's going on before their next nap.

> Nuka is a very expressive sleeper. Sometimes I can hear her from another floor of the house, whimpering and growling in her dreams. Other times, her tail thumps enthusiastically against the ground as she relives a happy experience. Her rear legs sometimes move so forcefully she looks like she's imitating a kangaroo. I would love to be able to peek inside her brain and find out what story is unfolding in there. Marlowe finds the whole thing tiresome, though. He often goes off to sleep in a different room so she doesn't interrupt his beauty rest.

What the happiness experts say

Sleep is essential for your mental and physical health, yet many people try to survive on less and less sleep in an effort to fit more work and other activities into their days. Modern society values being constantly busy and labels sleep as wasted time when nothing gets accomplished. Nothing could be further from the truth.

I won't go into all the negative effects of sleep deprivation, since that could fill an entire book. Let's just focus on how sleeping affects happiness. According to positive psychology expert Shawn Achor, your brain interprets a lack of sleep as a threat. Perhaps this is because our ancestors would have stayed awake only when they felt threatened by wild animals or other groups of humans who might attack during the night. In that state of mind, your brain is constantly scanning for bad stuff and doesn't have room to absorb positive thoughts.

Researchers who had people memorize lists of positive, neutral, and negative words before sleeping found that when the subjects were allowed to sleep for seven to eight hours, they remembered around the same number of words from each list the next day. If they were deprived of sleep, they remembered just as many negative and neutral words but far fewer of the positive words. It's like the lack of sleep acted as a filter, getting rid of anything positive in their brains. Imagine what this does to you if you're continually sleep-deprived.

People who haven't slept enough also produce more cortisol, which is a stress hormone. Your brain and body react as though something very stressful is happening to you, which of course affects your mood. That's why people are so grumpy when they haven't slept enough. It can also throw off the balance of other hormones, like the ones that control whether you feel hungry or full. Basically, when you're sleepy you constantly feel hungry, and you'll keep eating without ever feeling satisfied because your hormones don't tell you when you're full.

During sleep, your body repairs itself. It's when you build new muscle tissue, among other things. If you're hitting the gym regularly but not getting enough sleep, you're not going to get the results you're hoping for.

Social welfare expert Katherine Compitus says that when clients tell her they're having trouble focusing at work, or they're trying to lose weight and it's not working, she asks how much sleep they're getting. "I tell people that sleep is not wasted time. It's recharging your battery. If you don't recharge your battery, it's not going to work."

Your brain is very busy while you're sleeping. Sleep appears to play a central role in our ability to learn new things, remember things, and solve problems. There's a reason you sometimes wake up with a solution to something tricky that was bothering you the day before. When you "sleep on it," your brain works on the problem overnight while you're not even aware of it. Rather than *wasting* time while you sleep, you could actually be *saving* yourself a lot of time trying to work out complex problems. Sleep is when your brain makes new connections. If you're learning a new skill (or language or activity), you need to let those new neural connections form while you sleep or you won't retain everything you worked so hard to learn.

It's not just overnight slumber that affects your brain. A short nap can boost your creativity. The famous surrealist painter Salvador Dalí (the one with the melting clocks) used "micro naps" to spark creativity. He would fall asleep sitting in a chair while holding a metal spoon or a key. The moment he fell asleep, the object would fall from his hand and the noise it made hitting the ground would wake him up. When you wake up during the early sleep stage, known as the hypnagogic state, or N1, it gives you a creative boost that can help with anything from imagining new worlds to solving math problems. Inventor Thomas Edison was also a fan of micro napping.

> I sleep best when I'm on a backpacking trip. First, I'm doing physical work all day so I get tired at night. Second, there's no artificial light—once the sun is down, my body gets the hint that it's time to rest. Add a cozy sleeping bag and the fresh air blowing through the tent, and it's the perfect combination to make me doze off. And there may be another reason I sleep well when I'm camping—the usual stressors from my everyday life are gone. My mind has the time and space to shut down more fully at night. There's not much of this experience that I can bring into my regular nights to improve my sleep at home, but I can avoid too many bright lights before bedtime, let some fresh air into the house, and do my best not to think about work or to-do lists when I crawl under the covers.

How to be happier by curling up and sleeping

There are two main reasons that getting enough sleep will make you happier:

1. Prioritizing rest will force you to take a closer look at how you organize your time, decide what's truly important, and figure out what time-consuming things in your life don't make you happy, so you can eliminate them.

2. Your brain will be able to function properly so you can process your memories and emotions, let positive thoughts sink in, and keep your hormones balanced. Your body will also work better, meaning you'll get sick less often and heal faster, which makes it easier to be happy.

Prioritize rest

If you allow yourself to sleep only when you have nothing else to do, it's time to change that mentality and make sleep a priority. You schedule time to do your work, to be with family and friends, and to take care of your body (I hope)—you should also schedule your sleep time and stick to it.

Compitus suggests looking at sleeping as a skill you can work on—something few of us do. "We need to think of sleep as a healthy and adaptive skill. It's when our body does a lot of healing. Dreaming is also when we process a lot of information; whether it's a good dream or a bad dream, we kind of sort through all the busy stuff in our heads. It's incredibly healthy to sleep." She says that people have forgotten how to listen to their bodies. Instead of going to bed when they're tired, they watch more TV, or stay out for another drink, or try to get a little more work done. Your body tells you when it's time to sleep, but only if you're listening.

Prioritizing sleep isn't a selfish act. The truth is, you aren't going to be giving anyone else your best if you aren't sleeping well. By getting enough sleep, you increase the chances that you're going to be more friendly, helpful, creative, and productive. Happiness expert Stephanie Staples says that missing out on sleep makes it hard to be the person you want to be. "We can't be who we want for ourselves. We can't be who we want in our significant relationships. We can't be the parents that our kids deserve. We can't be the colleague that our colleagues deserve. We cannot function at our best at a very basic level if we are not getting adequate sleep."

How to sleep more

If you're like me, you might go to bed at a reasonable time with the best intentions of getting a solid eight hours of sleep, then find yourself lying there with your mind going a million miles an hour and getting more and more stressed about the fact that you aren't asleep yet. Thankfully, there are plenty of techniques to help you get to sleep at night. It might take a bit of experimentation to learn what works for you.

The first step is setting a consistent bedtime for yourself. Yes, there will be exceptions, but if you make a point of always going to bed at a certain time, your body will learn to wind down automatically at that time. Waking up at the same time every morning will help too. Sleeping in on the weekend, for example, might prevent you from feeling tired at your usual bedtime when Sunday night arrives.

An evening routine is also helpful. First, turn off your screens and put your phone down at least half an hour before you want to fall asleep, preferably longer. Blue light from screens can interfere with your brain's message that it's nighttime. Plus, if your mind is engaged in chatting with friends, catching up on your social media feed, or watching videos, you will have a harder time calming your thoughts when you climb into bed.

Second, go through the same pattern every night before bedtime. This reinforces habits, like you learned in "Learn new tricks." Your brain gets used to a sequence of events: check that your door is locked, brush your teeth, wash up, get changed, check your alarm, and so on. A nightly ritual makes it easier to relax because you're on autopilot; you won't stay up wondering if you've forgotten something important.

Third, calm your mind. This is where things come down to personal preference. Here are a few ideas that might work for you:

- Do some relaxation exercises or breathing exercises
- Meditate
- Gently stretch to release tension
- Write down your thoughts about the day in a journal
- Write a list of things to remember for tomorrow so you don't stay up worrying about them
- Write down or think about the good things that happened today
- Add slips of paper with your little success stories to a "win jar" that you open at the end of the year
- Write down or think about things you are grateful for
- Say a prayer
- Watch your children or pets sleep for a few minutes
- Listen to calming music or sounds, like waves on a beach or falling rain

Any of these practices can help put you in a more positive state of mind and keep you from feeling anxious or replaying negative experiences while you're trying to fall asleep.

Paws and reflect

- 🐾 Your brain sees a lack of sleep as a sign that you're in danger, so you get stressed and anxious if you don't sleep enough.
- 🐾 Sleep is important for processing memories, healing your body, keeping your immune system working, and even solving problems.
- 🐾 Getting enough sleep makes you happier because you'll lower your levels of stress hormones and have greater mental capacity to enjoy what you're doing and focus on it.
- 🐾 Schedule sleeping time rather than going to bed only when there's nothing else left to do.
- 🐾 Create an evening routine to help train your brain to calm down at night so you can fall asleep faster.

Photo credit: Katryn B. for Pixabay

16
Dig below the surface

Pawsitive dogma

The way your life appears at surface level can deceive you. If something you've buried deep down is standing in the way of your happiness, you need to discover what lies below.

Note from Nuka

Smelling stuff on the ground is good, but I want to find out more. Where is that smell coming from? Is there something under the dirt that I can't get at from here? What can I discover hiding down there if I dig down a little more?

People like to think they understand what's going on, but sometimes they're just seeing what's on the surface—the part everyone can see. It's not until you start digging *down deeper that you get the whole story and figure out what's making your life a bit stinky. You might need to deal with that stuff before you can really be happy.*

What the dog experts say

There are a few reasons why a dog might dig in the ground. First, they might be trying to dig their way out of a situation they are unhappy with, like when a dog digs under a fence to escape. Second, they might want to hide something away for later, like when a dog buries a bone. But most often, dogs dig because they believe there's something of interest below the surface and they want to uncover it.

As you found out in "Stop and smell things," dogs are incredibly good at picking up very subtle smells. Humans take advantage of this skill all the time by training dogs to identify certain smells and let us know when they find them. That could be the smell of drugs, money, truffles, explosives, or even cancer.

When it comes to buried things, dogs know just where to dig. Their sense of smell, and sometimes their hearing, can save human lives. Dogs are much faster at locating victims of avalanches and landslides than people are. Finding buried people faster is critical for saving them before they run out of air or become crushed under debris. Cadaver dogs can even locate people who have drowned from the smell that reaches the water's surface.

Dogs use their digging skills to help humans do all kinds of things, but of course those skills evolved in dogs for different reasons—mainly for finding food. Dogs can hear the tiny squeaks of rodents in underground burrows and dig to get them out. Dogs also dig up food buried by other dogs, as well as squirrels and other animals, who have hidden it away for later.

While dogs usually dig with a purpose in mind, we've selectively bred some dogs to enhance their digging behavior. As a result, there are dogs who just plain enjoy it. They use digging to burn off excess energy the way another dog might do zoomies around the yard or keep chasing a ball for as long as you're willing to throw it.

> When Marlowe smells something on the ground, he may scrape at the dirt a couple of times to stir up more of the scent. Nuka, on the other hand, is a digging machine! She'll dig a deep ditch in the ground in a matter of seconds. When she was a puppy, our yard looked like a war zone. We tried all the usual tricks to discourage her, like putting a rock in the hole or covering it with chicken wire. She'd just find a new spot and dig a new hole. Eventually we built a big sand pit in one corner of our yard and encouraged her to dig there. She caught on impressively fast, and now she digs in her pit for fun instead of destroying our lawn. I don't think she ever looks happier than when she's having a good dig.

What the happiness experts say

You might think you know what's going on in your own mind, but the truth is we spend most of our time dealing with surface-level stuff. Maybe you feel stressed out. Maybe your relationships aren't going well. There are a lot of things that can get in the way of feeling happy. But often the real cause is not obvious when you're looking at the surface—the way you feel and behave at the time. You may need to dig down to deeper levels to find out the real cause of your state of mind.

Many people feel uncomfortable doing that kind of digging, according to happiness coach Kim Strobel. "Many people live 'less than' lives because there's so much potential inside of them, but they're not willing to weed through and see what is there and what is the root cause [of their challenges]. I also don't think that we have deep conversations with others. I think it's all very surface level, many times. Dogs are willing to just keep digging until they find what they're looking for."

Trying to figure this stuff out for yourself is hard because you see only what you expect to see. Psychologist and dog behavior expert Alexandra Horowitz says this is called "inattentional blindness," meaning we don't see things unless we already expect to see them. "Attention and expectation also work together to oblige our missing things right in front of our noses. Part of what restricts us seeing things is that we have an expectation about what we will see, and we are actually perceptually restricted by that expectation. Expectation magically sorts the world into things-we-are-looking-for and things-we-are-not."

This applies to your beliefs as much as it does to actual things you can see and touch and experience. Thanks to confirmation bias, you pay more attention to things that support your existing view of the world, and you ignore or reject information that suggests your view is wrong. Combine this with negativity bias, and it becomes very hard to absorb information that suggests you could be happier than you currently are by making changes in your life. You might need someone else's help to point out what's holding you back.

Unfortunately, some people feel there's a stigma to seeking help—that it's admitting weakness and that people will think less of them. Happiness expert Stephanie Staples says, "I think when you ask for help, whether it's to get therapy or whatever it is, it's showing a sign of strength. I think you're in the top 3% of the population if you have the wherewithal to question some things, and to dig a little deeper and wonder. You're not just accepting everything at face value."

Strobel says that we can't always figure it out for ourselves because so much of what's happening in our minds is subconscious. "Only 5% of how we show up in our lives really comes from the conscious brain—the thinking brain, the logical, reasoning, rational brain. But the subconscious mind is kind of like the darkroom of the brain. It's where you hold all your beliefs and values. And what we know is that 95% of how you navigate life comes from the subconscious mind." If you're unhappy, it's quite likely that something in your life is offending your core beliefs and values. But unless you dig into those beliefs in detail, it could be very difficult to identify and resolve the problem. And until you resolve it, you will find it harder to be happy.

If you're feeling unfulfilled at home or at work, finding it hard to commit to a relationship, feeling anxious or stressed for no obvious reason, having trouble bouncing back from a bad experience, or just not feeling joyful even when things are going well, it might be time to dig a little deeper.

> I have a complicated relationship with my mirror. One morning, I'll stand in front of it in my underwear and think, "Hey, I'm looking good!" The next day, I'll stand in front of the same mirror, at the same time, in similar (but hopefully not the same) underwear and think, "Oh yuck, I look so fat!" Logically, I know I look exactly the same. And yet, on the second day my happiness will be affected by how I felt about my mirror image in the morning. What's going on?
>
> It took some introspection and mental digging to figure out that my mirror problem had nothing to do with my mirror image or how I actually looked that day. My self-image actually changes depending on whether I think I've been overeating recently, how my workouts are going, how things are going with my work, how good I feel about my marriage, and just about anything else. The surface issue of my mirror image is just how my deeper feelings of self-worth find their way into my conscious brain and express themselves.

How to be happier by digging below the surface

If you want to be happier, the first thing you need to do is prioritize the things that would make you happy. Makes sense, right? Most of us set goals that we think will get us closer to happiness, but this only works if you set the right goals. Maybe getting promoted at work sounds like a good goal, but is it really going to make you happier? Or will you just end up working more and having less time for the most important people in your life? You need to go back to what we discussed in "Learn new tricks" and start digging deeper into *why* you chose a particular goal.

Find your why

Fitness expert Oonagh Duncan says, "We usually lose sight of what we truly want. We think we want that sweet job or a million bucks or for George Clooney to give us a massage. But no, we want the feelings we think will ensue—in essence, happiness. Take any goal you have and ask yourself *why* enough times, and you will always get to *happiness*."

Look at the things you are prioritizing in your life and start digging into why those are your priorities. If the answer is "everyone expects me to" or "it's what you're supposed to do" or "it's always been that way," you might not be on the road to happiness. Shifting priorities is scary, especially if it might mean starting a new career or ending a relationship, but eventually you need to find the path where your why is "because it will make me happy."

Dig up the past

Other barriers to happiness can involve issues from your past that you haven't fully moved beyond. Even things that happened years ago can prevent you from feeling truly happy today. Positive neuroplasticity expert Rick Hanson says people are often frustrated that old problems still bother them. "Many people are embarrassed about 'still carrying the past.' They ask, why haven't I gotten over this by now, what's wrong with me? But the brain is designed to be continually remodeled by experiences in ways that last. If we can be changed for the better in life, we must also be changeable for the worse; in fact, the brain's negativity bias makes us especially changeable by negative experiences. Your personal history matters, it has consequences. It can leave you with a hole in your heart."

Finding out what's below the surface, causing your ongoing stress, anxiety, or sadness, can be unpleasant. Therapists specialize in uncovering the past causes of your issues and helping you understand them better. They can provide support to help you move on with your life in a more positive state of mind, letting your happiness grow.

Social welfare expert Katherine Compitus understands that taking this step is difficult for a lot of her therapy clients. "Sometimes people are scared, with good reason, to search for the cause. But, certainly, we do not heal if we don't search for the cause. If we learn how to reflect, if we let ourselves be vulnerable to ourselves—or to a therapist, a dog, a friend, a pastor, whoever it is—we can look at why we are doing certain behaviors, and what's the consequence or the result." She says that once you bring the events in your past to the surface, you can begin to find ways to change your perspective and move on. "We cannot change the facts of a situation, but we can change the way we think about them. When we have that insight, when we can see we're doing this behavior, we can catch ourselves and say, 'All right, that's one way of thinking about it. What's another way of thinking about it?'"

If you've been trying to use the tips in this book to increase your happiness, but you can't seem to shift your mood or create more positive thoughts, perhaps you need to dig deeper. Getting another perspective can be the first step toward healing from the past and becoming ready to embrace happiness.

Paws and reflect

- 🐾 You may not see the real reasons why you are not feeling happy. People tend to see only what they expect to see, and other information goes unnoticed. An outside perspective might help you see what you're missing.

- 🐾 When you look at your goals and activities, ask yourself why you have chosen to do those things. Are you spending most of your time trying to meet society's expectations or please others instead of doing what will make you happier?

- 🐾 Issues from your past can weigh down your mind and make it difficult to feel happy. You may need to think differently about past issues and experiences to help you move past them.

Photo credit: Monica Laane-Fralick "Georgie"

Stay pawsitive!

Pawsitive dogma

Happiness does not come from knowing. It can only be found by doing and being.

Message from Marlowe and Nuka

Hey, thanks for reading our book! It's been hard work giving you all this advice, but if it helps you to be happy like us it was worth it. We hope we did a good job of explaining how we stay happy most of the time, and how you can do that too if you follow our example. We love it when our people are happy because it means they feel like playing more and doing lots of fun stuff. So please keep practicing being happy, and we think that before long it will be your normal way to be. Most of all—stay pawsitive!

How to be as happy as your dog

There are undoubtedly more than 16 ways that adopting a more dog-like attitude can make you happier, but hopefully you're off to a good start. If you're looking for more inspiration, pay close attention when you're around your dog (or any happy dog).

I began this exploration of how to become happier with learning new tricks. That's because everything else in the book can only help you become happier if you're willing and able to make some changes in your life, including to your point of view.

I finished with a focus on digging below the surface for similar reasons. If there's something buried deep inside preventing you from embracing the ideas in this book, you may not be able to find true happiness until you uncover the experiences and emotions that are holding you back.

If you've made it this far, my hope is that you've found some ideas that will add more happiness to your life. Remember, you don't need to do every single thing I've suggested, and there's no set order to do them in. Start with some easy wins—whatever you can add to your routine right away—and then add some more challenging changes that could make a significant difference to your mood and your lifestyle.

If you haven't already done this, make a list of a few things you can start doing immediately. Maybe it's going to bed earlier, adding more playtime into your schedule, savoring some of the good experiences in your life, or stopping to "smell" things more often. Or perhaps you want to start by considering whether your current pack is making you happy. Did anything in the book give you an "aha!" moment? Whatever suggestions appealed to you the most are the ones you're most likely to stick with. Just pursue your happiness and make it a priority!

Whenever making these positive changes seems difficult, turn to your favorite four-legged role model for emotional support, an instant mood boost, and an active demonstration of what happiness looks like. Your dog would never consider it "too hard" to be happy, and neither should you. Enjoy some cuddles and treats, wag your tail, and decide that it's time to be as happy as your dog.

Selected bibliography

If you're interested in reading any of the books I've mentioned or quoted from, use the information here to find them at your local bookstore or library.

Dogs

Berns, Gregory. *What It's Like to Be a Dog* (New York: Basic Books, 2017).

Bradshaw, John. *Dog Sense* (New York: Basic Books, 2011).

Coren, Stanley. *Do Dogs Dream?* (New York: W.W. Norton, 2012).

Coren, Stanley. *How Dogs Think* (New York: Free Press, 2004).

Coren, Stanley. *How to Speak Dog* (New York: Fireside, 2000).

Coren, Stanley. *Why Does My Dog Act That Way?* (New York: Atria Books, 2007).

Dunbar, Ian. *Dog Behavior* (New York: Howell Book House, 1999).

Grimm, David. *Citizen Canine* (New York: Public Affairs, 2014).

Horowitz, Alexandra. *Inside of a Dog* (New York: Scribner, 2009).

Happiness

Achor, Shawn. *Before Happiness* (New York: Crown Publishing, 2013).

Brown, Stuart. *Play* (New York: Penguin, 2009).

Duncan, Oonagh. *Healthy as F*ck* (Toronto: Penguin, 2019).

Eyre, Richard. *The Happiness Paradigm* (Sanger, CA: Familius, 2019).

Grenville-Cleave, Bridget. *Positive Psychology: A Toolkit for Happiness, Purpose and Well-Being* (London: Icon Books, 2016).

Haidt, Jonathan. *The Happiness Hypothesis* (New York: Basic Books, 2006).

Hanson, Rick. *Hardwiring Happiness* (New York: Harmony Books, 2013).

Horowitz, Alexandra. *On Looking* (New York: Scribner, 2013).

Ricard, Matthieu. *Happiness* (New York: Little, Brown, 2006).

Seligman, Martin. *Flourish* (New York: Atria Books, 2012).

Seppälä, Emma. *The Happiness Track: How to Apply the Science of Happiness to Accelerate Your Success* (New York: Harper One, 2017).

Notes

Introduction

83% of pet owners refer to themselves as "mom" or "dad." David Grimm, *Citizen Canine* (New York: Public Affairs, 2014), p. 12.

Researchers have shown that dogs can improve your health. Grimm, *Citizen Canine*, p. 224.

Dogs' brains have the same structures and functions as ours. Gregory Berns, *What It's Like to Be a Dog* (New York: Basic Books, 2017), p. 7.

Dogs produce the same hormones and undergo the same chemical changes as people. Stanley Coren, *Do Dogs Dream?* (New York: W.W. Norton, 2012), p. 50.

People have a negativity bias. Kim Strobel, interview.

Positive psychology was popularized by Martin Seligman. Bridget Grenville-Cleave, *Positive Psychology: A Toolkit for Happiness, Purpose and Well-Being* (London: Icon Books, 2016), p. 13.

Baseline happiness level. Grenville-Cleave, *Positive Psychology*, p. 24; Kim Strobel, interview.

Chapter 1

Owner contact is rewarding. John Bradshaw, *Dog Sense* (New York: Basic Books, 2011), p. 105. Reprinted by permission of Basic Books, an imprint of Hachette Book Group, Inc.

New is interesting. Alexandra Horowitz, *Inside of a Dog* (New York: Scribner, 2009), p. 289.

Training in different contexts. Nicole Barnett, interview.

40% of your happiness is determined by your actions and attitude. Grenville-Cleave, *Positive Psychology*, p. 4, discussing Sonja Lyubomirsky, Kennon M Sheldon, and David Schkade, "Pursuing Happiness: The Architecture of Sustainable Change," *Review of General Psychology* 9, no. 2 (2005): 111-131.

Go with the flow. Oonagh Duncan, *Healthy as F*ck* (Toronto: Penguin, 2019), p. 22. Reprinted by permission of Penguin Canada, a division of Penguin Random House Canada Limited. All rights reserved.

We feel gratified. Jonathan Haidt, *The Happiness Hypothesis* (New York: Basic Books, 2006), p. 97.

Flow. Mihaly Csikszentmihalyi, *Finding Flow: The Psychology of Engagement with Everyday Life* (New York: Basic Books, 1997).

Building new habits and skills. Duncan, *Healthy as F*ck*, p. 25-26. Reprinted by permission of Penguin Canada, a division of Penguin Random House Canada Limited. All rights reserved.

Chapter 2

Humans clog up their brains. Ian Dunbar, *Dog Behavior* (New York: Howell Book House, 1999), p. 16.

Sense of time is less sophisticated. Bradshaw, *Dog Sense*, p. 212. Reprinted by permission of Basic Books, an imprint of Hachette Book Group, Inc.

Harvard study. Matthew Killingsworth and Daniel Gilbert, "A Wandering Mind Is an Unhappy Mind," *Science* 330, no. 6006 (2010): 932. doi: 10.1126/science.1192438

Benefits of meditation. Grenville-Cleave, *Positive Psychology*, p. 129-130.

Savoring. Grenville-Cleave, *Positive Psychology*, p. 207.

Rewiring our brains. Rick Hanson, *Hardwiring Happiness* (New York: Harmony Books, 2013), p. 17.

Chapter 3

Dogs wag at things that are alive. Coren, *Do Dogs Dream?*, p. 106.

Wolf tail postures. Horowitz, *Inside of a Dog*, p. 112.

Dogs with docked tails fight more, Pauline C Bennett and Eloise Perini, "Tail Docking in Dogs: A Review of the Issues," *Australian Vet Journal* 81, no. 4 (2003): 208-218.

Frequency of positive thoughts. Grenville-Cleave, *Positive Psychology*, p. 36.

Recapture how you felt as a child. Grenville-Cleave, *Positive Psychology*, p. 210.

Chapter 4

Enriched social and physical environment for puppies. Dunbar, *Dog Behavior*, p. 52.

Without play signals, a bit is a bite. Horowitz, *Inside of a Dog*, p. 200.

Coyotes play by social rules. Grimm, *Citizen Canine*, p. 76.

Playing is more important than winning. Horowitz, *Inside of a Dog*, p. 197.

Play and happiness are linked in dogs. Bradshaw, *Dog Sense*, p. 169. Reprinted by permission of Basic Books, an imprint of Hachette Book Group, Inc.

Play promotes brain growth. Stuart Brown, *Play* (New York: Penguin, 2009), p. 48.

Play prevents dementia. Brown, *Play*, p. 58.

When deprived of play, we can't experience lasting pleasure. Brown, *Play*, p. 43.

Play is critical for happiness. Brown, *Play*, p. 6.

Play helps us connect with the best in ourselves. Brown, *Play*, p. 218.

Just watching dogs play has a mood- and body-altering effect. Brown, "The Science Behind ... Dog Parks," *Playcore* (blog), 4 February 2021. https://www.playcore.com/news/the-science-behind-dog-parks

Chapter 5

Wolf packs are cooperative. Bradshaw, *Dog Sense*, p. 147.

Dogs can create two sets of social connections in their brains. Bradshaw, *Dog Sense*, p. 212. Reprinted by permission of Basic Books, an imprint of Hachette Book Group, Inc.

Dogs have similar emotions to ours. Coren, *Do Dogs Dream?*, p. 50.

Around 47% of US adults are chronically lonely. John Murphy, "New Epidemic Affects Nearly Half of American Adults," MDLinx, 25 March 2020. https://www.mdlinx.com/article/new-epidemic-affects-nearly-half-of-american-adults/lfc-3272

Good social connections made people happier than money, success, or possessions; having a happy friend increases your probability of being happy. Grenville-Cleave, *Positive Psychology*, p. 50, referring to Ed Diener and Martin EP Seligman, "Very Happy People," *Psychological Science* 13 (2002): 81-84.

Giving feels better than getting support. Shawn Achor, *Before Happiness* (New York: Crown Publishing, 2013), p. 144, 146.

Chapter 6

Dogs can smell fear. Horowitz, *Inside of a Dog*, p. 80, 81.

Dogs can read their owner's thoughts. Dunbar, *Dog Behavior*, p. 18.

We have a like-o-meter. Haidt, *The Happiness Hypothesis*, p. 26.

We have a built-in empathy system. Emma Seppälä, *The Happiness Track: How to Apply the Science of Happiness to Accelerate Your Success* (New York: Harper One, 2017), ch. 6.

Walk with a physician, Alexandra Horowitz, *On Looking* (New York: Scribner, 2013), p. 181.

Powerful subconscious response to memory triggers. Katherine Compitus, interview.

Chapter 7

Stages of aggression. Stanley Coren, *Why Does My Dog Act That Way?* (New York: Atria Books, 2007), p. 150.

Distinctive barks. Horowitz, *Inside of a Dog*, p. 107.

Anger can build up under pressure. Bridget Grenville-Cleave, *Positive Psychology*, p. 113.

Suppressing negative emotions makes you feel more of them. James J Gross, "Emotion Regulation: Affective, Cognitive, and Social Consequences," *Psychophysiology* 39, no. 3 (2002): 281-291. doi: 10.1017.S0048577201393198.

Chapter 8

Dogs are ready to move on to something new. Horowitz, *Inside of a Dog*, p. 113.

Puppies need to recover quickly. Dunbar, *Dog Behavior*, p. 55.

Humans are prone to retaliation. Christopher Boehm, "Ancestral Hierarchy and Conflict," *Science* 336 (2012): 844-847.

Trying not to think about something backfires. Haidt, *The Happiness Hypothesis*, p. 19-23.

Antelope are resilient because they quickly change back to rest and digest mode. Seppälä, *The Happiness Track*, ch. 2.

Breathing exercises lower stress hormones. Seppälä, *The Happiness Track*, ch. 2.

Distractions can help you get into a positive mood. Grenville-Cleave, *Positive Psychology*, p. 30-31.

Chapter 9

The walk your dog wants. Horowitz, *Inside of a Dog*, p. 285.

Add some doggie parkour. Nicole Barnett, interview.

Dogs establish their place in the world. Stanley Coren, interview.

Moving your body makes you feel better mentally. Kim Strobel, interview.

Effects of physical exercise on the brain. Grenville-Cleave, *Positive Psychology*, p. 186.

Effects of a nature walk on the brain. Gregory N Bratman et al., "The Benefits of Nature Experience: Improved Affect and Cognition," *Landscape and Urban Planning* 138 (2014): 41-50. doi: 10.016/jlandurbplan.2015.02.005

People scored higher on creativity tests after a walk. Daniel L Schwartz, "Give Your Ideas Some Legs: The Positive Effect of Walking on Creative Thinking," *Journal of Experimental Psychology* 40, no. 4 (2014): 1142-1152.

Time away from work makes you more productive. Seppälä, *The Happiness Track*, ch. 3.

Chapter 10

Dogs have far more scent receptors than humans. Stanley Coren, interview.

Dogs have a vomeronasal organ. Horowitz, *Inside of a Dog*, p. 73.

Dogs have a 40% larger scent-processing area in their brains. Stanley Coren, interview.

Dogs likely memorize the scent of other dogs. Bradshaw, *Dog Sense*, p. 242.

A wholly new street after six hours. Horowitz, *On Looking*, p. 255.

Time spent going to and fro is forgotten. Horowitz, *On Looking*, p. 2.

Your brain receives 11 million bits of information per second but can process only 40. Manfred Zimmermann, "Neurophysiology of Sensory Systems" in *Fundamentals of Sensory Physiology*, 3rd rev. ed., ed. Robert F Schmidt (New York: Springer, 1986), p. 116.

Running events are about more than the finishing time. Stephanie Staples, interview.

You can change how you feel by changing the story you tell. Grenville-Cleave, *Positive Psychology*, p. 78.

Chapter 11

Rachel Friedman, "What Is a Treat? What Isn't?" *Dog Star Daily*, 15 October 2008. https://www.dogstardaily.com/blogs/what-treat-what-isn039t.

Police dogs are rewarded with a toy. Sean Thrush, interview.

There's a pitcher of water to refill the glass. Achor, *Before Happiness*, p. 36.

Self-control is like a muscle. Roy F Baumeister et al., "The Strength Model of Self-Control," *Current Directions in Psychological Science* 16, no. 6 (2007): 351-355.

Variety is the spice of life. Haidt, *The Happiness Hypothesis*, p. 96.

Research on basking in your pleasure. Fred B Bryant, "A Four-Factor Model of Perceived Control: Avoiding, Coping, Obtaining, and Savoring," *Journal of Personality* 57, no. 4 (1989). doi: 10.1111/j.1467-6494.1989.tb00494.x

Chapter 12

Research from Duke Canine Cognition Center. Grimm, *Citizen Canine*, p. 68, 71.

Self-criticism is harmful. Seppälä, *The Happiness Track*, ch. 5.

Negative thoughts lead to negative behavior. Duncan, *Healthy as F*ck*, p. 46. Reprinted by permission of Penguin Canada, a division of Penguin Random House Canada Limited. All rights reserved.

We take the positive things about ourselves for granted. Seppälä, *The Happiness Track*, ch. 5.

Annual review at work. Hanson, *Hardwiring Happiness*, p. 21.

Practice feeling sexy, confident, and happy. Duncan, *Healthy as F*ck*, p. 44.

Think about the things you're good at. Hanson, *Hardwiring Happiness*, p. 98.

Chapter 13

Dogs fetch as part of natural pack behavior and because of selective breeding. Bradshaw, *Dog Sense*, p. 105.

Chasing is part of a dog's hunting instincts. Stanley Coren, interview.

Some dogs prefer to play "keep-away" with the toy. Nicole Barnett, interview.

Mihaly Csikszentmihalyi flow research. Mihaly Csikszentmihalyi, "Go With the Flow," *Wired*, September 1996.

Pre-goal attainment positive affect and post-goal attainment positive affect. Richard J Davidson, "Affective Style and Affective Disorders: Perspectives from Affective Neuroscience," *Cognition and Emotion* 12, no. 3 (1998): 307-330.

Pleasure is momentary and external; happiness is internal and long lasting. Duncan, *Healthy as F*ck*, p. 54-55.

We adapt to things and start taking them for granted. Grenville-Cleave, *Positive Psychology*, p. 24.

Making old things seem new provides a dopamine hit. Wulfram Gerstner, Henning Sprekeler, and Gustavo Deco, "Theory and Simulation in Neuroscience," *Science* 338 (2012): 60-65.

Build up your capacity to be satisfied and your sense of feeling satisfied. Hanson, *Hardwiring Happiness*, p. 190.

Chapter 14

Dogs will chase something that's running away. Bradshaw, *Dog Sense*, p. 114.

Definition of happiness. Achor, *Before Happiness*, p. 107.

People in the same circumstances create different realities. Achor, *Before Happiness*, p. 13-14.

Approach goals are helpful but avoidance goals are not. Grenville-Cleave, *Positive Psychology*, p. 151.

You should look back at how far you've come. Minjung Koo and Ayelet Fishbach, "Dynamics of Self-Regulation: How (Un)accomplished Goal Actions Affect Motivation," *Journal of Personality and Social Psychology* 94, no. 2 (2008): 183-195.

Ask what action you will take each day. Achor, *Before Happiness*, p. 160.

Your brain releases chemicals when you believe you will reach your goal. Achor, *Before Happiness*, p. 166.

Chapter 15

Dogs need sleep for the same basic reasons as people. Michael J Breus, "How Much Do Dogs Sleep?" *The Sleep Doctor*, 30 June 2022. https://thesleepdoctor.com/animal-sleep-habits/how-much-do-dogs-sleep/

Dogs sleep around half the day. Breus, "How Much Do Dogs Sleep?"

Dogs dream about their usual activities. Coren, *Do Dogs Dream?*, p. 90.

Your brain interprets a lack of sleep as a threat. Achor, *Before Happiness*, p. 75.

Sleep deprivation filters out positive emotions and keeps negative ones. Matthew P Walker, "The Role of Sleep in Cognition and Emotion," *Annals of the New York Academy of Sciences* 1156 (2009): 168-197; Els van der Helm and Matthew P Walker, "Overnight Therapy: The Role of Sleep in Emotional Brain Processing," PubMed Central, 23 June 2010. www.ncbi.nlm.nih.gov/pmc/articles/PMC2890316/

Lack of sleep produces cortisol and throws off your other hormone balances. Duncan, *Healthy as F*ck*, p. 92.

Salvador Dalí used "micro naps" to spark creativity. Yasemin Saplakoglu, "Sleep Technique Used by Salvador Dalí Really Works," *Live Science*, 8 December 2021. https://www.livescience.com/little-known-sleep-stage-may-be-creative-sweet-spot

Turn off your screens at night. Michelle Drerup, "Why You Should Ditch Your Phone Before Bed," *Cleveland Clinic Health Essentials*, 20 May 2022. https://health.clevelandclinic.org/put-the-phone-away-3-reasons-why-looking-at-it-before-bed-is-a-bad-habit/

Chapter 16

Dogs have several reasons for digging. Nicole Barnett, interview.

Dogs can find buried humans. Dunbar, *Dog Behavior*, p. 16.

We don't see things unless we're looking for them. Horowitz, *On Looking*, p. 122-124.

You pay more attention to things that support your existing view. Hanson, *Hardwiring Happiness*, p. 24.

People are embarrassed about carrying the past. Hanson, *Hardwiring Happiness*, p. 153.

Acknowledgments

I must begin by acknowledging the huge roles that Marlowe and Nuka play in this book. I would like to think that if they had any idea what a book is, they would approve of this one in particular. They are slightly annoyed that they didn't get co-author credits, but they have decided to let it slide since the book is dedicated to them. I'd also like to thank all the other dogs who have helped me learn so much about happiness throughout my life, including my childhood dogs, Terry and Sniffer.

Thanks to my husband, Gerhard, for being supportive whenever I have a crazy idea for a book, whether it leads to a dead end (as some have) or becomes an actual published work.

This book draws on the work of many people with a huge range of expertise in dog and human behavior. I greatly appreciate the thoughtful input of the experts who made time to speak with me: Nicole Barnett, Dr. Katherine Compitus, Dr. Stanley Coren, Stephanie Staples, and Kim Strobel. Thanks also to Officer Sean Thrush who spoke to me about police dogs for an earlier project.

I'm also grateful for the support of my editorial dream team: Jess Shulman, Patricia MacDonald, and Ann Kennedy. It was such a treat to be able to handpick the people who would usher my book through the process and make it better with every step. Thanks to Michelle Fairbanks of Fresh Design and Sophie Hanks for making the book shelf-ready (and e-reader ready). And I am very thankful for my incredibly supportive mastermind group, who kept pushing me forward throughout this process.

Thank you to my amazing friends and family for cheering me on as my writing career has taken various surprising twists and turns. You lift me up when I'm down and give me confidence when I'm unsure. I couldn't do this without you.

Fifty-one beautiful, happy dogs were entered in a photo contest to grace the cover of this book. I appreciate everyone who took the time to enter and vote. It was extremely difficult to choose just one!

I'd also like to take this opportunity to thank the many, many people who work (often unpaid) to rescue dogs and other animals all around the world. It's sometimes overwhelming to think about how many animals are in need of a safe home, and those of you with the fortitude and generosity of spirit to do something about it have my endless admiration.

If you are adding a dog to your family, please adopt, don't shop.

About the author

Michelle Waitzman is a writer, plain language consultant, and dog lover. She is also the author of *Sex in a Tent: A Wild Couple's Guide to Getting Naughty in Nature*, *Moon: Living Abroad in New Zealand*, and *Psychic Animals: Superstition, Science and Extraordinary Tales*. Before her writing career, Michelle worked in TV production and corporate communications. She lives with her husband and two mixed-breed rescue dogs, Marlowe and Nuka, in Toronto, Canada.

Photo credit: Gerhard Pretorius

CPSIA information can be obtained
at www.ICGtesting.com
Printed in the USA
LVHW082052180423
744638LV00009B/130